...And The Tardy Bell Rings

JADA LEDFORD DAVES

KENDALL/HUNT PUBLISHING COMPANY
4050 Westmark Drive   Dubuque, Iowa 52002

This book is based on a true story, with actual incidents involving real people. However, the names of most of the people and places have been changed to protect the privacy of the individuals concerned.

Dedication

To my best friend and spouse Kevin—thanks for all your patience in helping me through this most difficult first year of teaching—and for your encouragement to write the book. It would not have been possible without you.

Acknowledgments

Many thanks to:

- ➤ My parents, Don and Wilby Ledford, for they have been my greatest teachers in life

- ➤ My high school home economics teachers, Mrs. John Anna Hunt and Mrs. Renee Webb, for without their example, I might have never chosen teaching as a profession

- ➤ Sheila Smith, for helping implant the idea for this book in my brain

- ➤ My brother, John Ledford, for his encouragement and help in hooking me up with Brenda Hunter, who in turn, led me to my publishing company

- ➤ Helen Bates, for telling my mother about the writing class which inspired me to "go finish the book"

- ➤ Dr. Cliff Schimmels, for helping to make this book a reality through many hours of reading my manuscript and "coaching" me to the next step

- ➤ Becky Dethero, for giving her time to consult with me about her experiences as a freelance writer

- ➤ Dr. Sally Young, Associate Professor of English at the University of Tennessee at Chattanooga, for her guidance in the documentation and proofreading process

- ➤ Ray Hall, for his assistance with some of my research

- ➤ All of my students, my basketball girls, my principal, other administrators in the school system, and to the entire community that nurtured me throughout this experience

- ➤ My faithful editor, Alex Chambliss, who made this experience such a time of learning and fun

- ➤ My wonderful husband Kevin, who has been my steadfast companion throughout this whole process

- ➤ My Heavenly Father, who gave me the strength and courage to see this project completed

Table of Contents

Introduction

As I sit here in total exasperation, my mind, soul and body wonder how I ever completed this book. How did it get started? From what idea or thought did this book spring?

In the early fall of my 1992-93 year as a "rookie" teacher, I met a bright, enthusiastic lady who served as support services director for the county in which I was teaching.

She dropped by to discuss a few things with me and, as we began to share some common concerns about education, she said, "Jada, you must keep a journal of the happenings that take place this year. Please take a few minutes each day to record events, ideas, and special memories. You'll be glad you did. I wish I had done this twenty-five years ago when I first started teaching. You never know, one day you may even write a book."

After her advice, I began to chew on the idea of actually writing a book. What could be more challenging, more exciting, than to express on paper what teaching is really all about?

I wrote this book for two reasons. First, to be a helpmeet for those attempting to pursue a career in education. Secondly, I wanted to share some heartwarming stories about my experiences as a part of a wonderful, small-town community.

Whiteville, Tennessee is home to some 2,200 people. It was born as a coal mining town, but most of the residents now commute to jobs in the big city.

A good bit of the activity in the community centers around Whiteville High. Students and their families are very involved in supporting school-related activities, as there's not much else to do in town. It was a marvelous place to begin my career in teaching.

I chose the book's title, ... *And the Tardy Bell Rings,* because of the relevance each day's tardy bell had on my first year.

When the tardy bell rings students are to be in class, in their seats, with supplies in hand—ready to start work. If they're not, they are marked as tardy for that particular class. And, in most school systems, three tardies is the equivalent of an absence, so it's very important to be on time and to be prepared.

The lifestyle of a first-year teacher is much like that of the student who comes in tardy and unprepared for the events of the day.

My first year was hectic. I was rushing to make it to class on time, get forms completed and turned in to the office, serve on hall duty, organize classroom events, get papers graded and finish make-up work—not to mention trying to keep my sanity.

The tension and excitement, which sometimes gave me stomachaches and headaches, were the problems of a first-year teacher hoping to make it to class before the tardy bell rang.

It was a constant race to be at the right place at the right time with the right information for the right students. Whew! And that was before trying to function soundly enough to present a strong educational and motivating lecture or activity.

Each day, with each new lesson, was like entering a den of lions—only to possibly be devoured. Even with nerves on edge, it was a magical thrill to successfully complete another day in this whole new world of teaching.

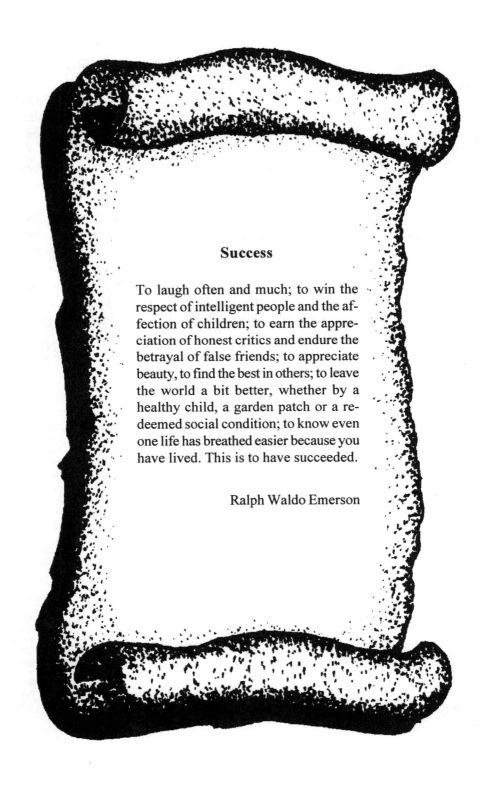

Success

To laugh often and much; to win the respect of intelligent people and the affection of children; to earn the appreciation of honest critics and endure the betrayal of false friends; to appreciate beauty, to find the best in others; to leave the world a bit better, whether by a healthy child, a garden patch or a redeemed social condition; to know even one life has breathed easier because you have lived. This is to have succeeded.

Ralph Waldo Emerson

Help Me Find My Place in This World

1

It was January—cold, rainy and very foggy; a perfect day for curling up by the fire and doing nothing. Nevertheless, I forced myself out of my warm bed to face another dreaded day of this "fantastic" career I wished I could turn my back on.

I needed to pull myself together so I wouldn't project my depressed attitude to my students. I put on my favorite CD to "pump me up" but that didn't work. I rambled to the kitchen for my favorite breakfast, but it just didn't satisfy. I took an extra-long, hot shower to relax my tired, aching body, but the muscles only tightened. I put on my favorite outfit and earrings, only to feel less attractive and confident than I ever had before.

Why was I so confused? Why did I feel this way?

With each passing day I thought things would get better. I had been a teacher for a little more than four months and I was already counting the days till spring break. My emotional being was exhausted. I was unsatisfied and very unfulfilled, but I pressed on.

As I drove to work, I tried to reflect on the joys of teaching. It might have been a bad time for thoughts on the subject, but nothing came to mind. During my regular 35-minute, one-way trip to the small country school where I taught, I was overwhelmed at the mess in which I found myself.

"I can start back to school this summer and go into another field," I repeated aloud to myself over the music on the radio. But just as I was feeling a bit of hope, I saw the entrance sign "Whiteville High School" to remind me of the long six months ahead.

I somehow managed to drag myself out of the car and make my way into the school. I was greeted by an office filled with colleagues, students, parents, and administrators.

"Good morning, Jada."

"Hey Jada! I love that blazer ... Oh, and the purse ... Is it new? ... It looks great."

"Jada, how are things going? Big game tonight ... What's the outlook for the girls?"

"Miss Ledford, I've been looking all over for you. I wanted to turn in my project early. I worked on it till midnight. It's so neat ... and I learned so much. I wanted to give it to you so you could start grading it. Thanks. See you in class!"

Being bombarded with all these questions, getting compliments, realizing someone was actually concerned about my opinion, and seeing the glow of an eager student's face after she has completed her assignment made me smile and soothed my whipped body.

These people truly cared about me in a way I had never realized before. We were family. My fellow teachers and I went through the same struggles day-in and day-out, but continued because of our mission to help, nurture and teach young people.

I was not alone in my chaotic world—there were many others— and if they could bear the load then I could, too.

One of my greatest struggles has been deciding on a career that fits my lifestyle. How do I make such a crucial decision? What if my decision is wrong?

As a small child, I found myself flipping through the Sears, Roebuck and Co. catalog. Especially at Christmastime, I would ask my parents for several of the "dress up" costumes.

One year I would be a ballerina, another year a model, and the next a firefighter. I would always tell my parents, "When I grow up I want to be a ____," and within a few days (sometimes weeks) I had completely changed my mind.

It wasn't long after this stage that I began taking lessons. I started mimicking the characters I wanted to be. I took piano for eight years, hoping one day to be a famous pianist. I took ballerina lessons, tap, jazz and baton, hoping one day to be a dancer, performer, or the like. Voice instruction, along with drama and theater classes at area colleges, quickly followed. I would be a young, aspiring actress in Hollywood and make lots of money for everyone to enjoy, I thought.

Then came athletic practices. Junior pro basketball, T-league baseball and swimming. I'm not sure if I realized that sports were not a promising future for a female, but I enjoyed them all the same. These experiences were building discipline and character traits that would define my being. So, I dreamed on.

In junior high, I thought I would live forever with my mother and father. Even the mention of work sent chills up my spine. I was lazy and I loved it. If I had to exert any amount of energy toward anything other than answering and talking on the telephone, I wasn't interested. My world was just me and my clique of girlfriends, and we had that world by the tail.

High school quickly approached. As a freshman, I realized I must "hit the books" in order to succeed and complete my education. By the end of my sophomore year, I imagined a career as a doctor, a lawyer—someone who makes big money.

The guidance counselor warned me that advanced science and math classes were prerequisites for medical school. Nightmares of chemistry, physics, trigonometry and calculus ran through my mind. And I remember telling her, "I think I'll choose another career." But I did struggle through some of those courses so I would have a "safety cushion," and I lived to see graduation day.

Then it was off to college. Planning my college career was like organizing my own funeral. I was afraid, lonely and felt as if I had no control over my decisions.

I thought, "What if I change majors six or eight times like my friends have? What if I choose a major just for the sake of making a commitment and somehow convincing my parents that I won't make a career out of college? How will I ever know if my choice was best for me?"

College life flew by. Once my degree was in hand and I entered the work force, doubts and fears began to creep in. "Did I make a mistake? Have I specialized in a field where I'm unhappy and disillusioned?"

Growing up, I always idolized teachers. Teachers were heroes to me and I hoped that one day I could walk in their shoes.

I had a stay-at-home mom, a situation that helped give me a strong family background. My family was everything to me. My mom taught me the basic fundamentals in life—and to her I will always be grateful.

I was better prepared for kindergarten than most children. My mom had already taught me the alphabet, how to tell time, how to tie my shoes...I was farther along than my peers. Also, my social development was above and beyond my screaming-and-kicking, crying-and-clinging-to-mama's-leg counterparts.

School was fun for me. In kindergarten, I looked forward to greeting Mrs. Crawford every morning and meeting up with my friends. I couldn't wait to work on math, do science experiments, cook something tasty in the kitchen, or jump rope and play ball at recess.

Life was challenging to me. The world was broad in scope, but I was determined to make myself someone extraordinarily special.

Nap time was a real bore. Who had time to sleep with so many things to explore? I was not a good nap taker, and soon my parents were convinced of this.

My father chose to pick me up from kindergarten at 1:30, so I wouldn't have to stay through naptime and leave at 3:00 with the other kids.

Jealousy is not a strong enough word to describe how my friends felt. How could Jada be so lucky as to leave before naptime? I'm not sure myself, but did I ever enjoy it!

After school, I would spend the rest of my day with my dad. He would take me down to the local snack bar and I would order french fries and a soft drink. Then we would go to his office, where my afternoon would be spent as a "helper" until mom arrived at 3:00.

My parents also extended my world by giving me extra responsibilities at home, and all of the opportunities they gave me as a youngster were crucial in my developmental process.

I learned very early to take hold of life's opportunities and make something out of them. I also learned that I did not want to be like everyone else.

I wanted to create my own utopia with my God-given talents and abilities. Being a leader and taking responsibility were two things I thrived on.

I started to dream of a career that would allow me to help others. I wanted to be a positive influence on others, and I was going to find a way to do it.

I began to see myself as a role model for teenagers. I was sure that my "calling" was to work with thirteen- to eighteen-year-old kids. And, I quickly realized, this was going to be a rather difficult goal.

Life means making tough decisions and living with them, whether they're good or bad. I was inspired in high school to pursue a career as an educator.

And here I am.

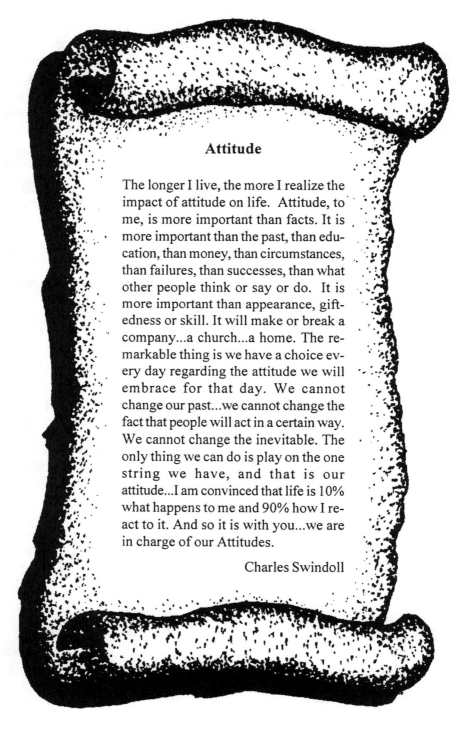

Attitude

The longer I live, the more I realize the impact of attitude on life. Attitude, to me, is more important than facts. It is more important than the past, than education, than money, than circumstances, than failures, than successes, than what other people think or say or do. It is more important than appearance, giftedness or skill. It will make or break a company...a church...a home. The remarkable thing is we have a choice every day regarding the attitude we will embrace for that day. We cannot change our past...we cannot change the fact that people will act in a certain way. We cannot change the inevitable. The only thing we can do is play on the one string we have, and that is our attitude...I am convinced that life is 10% what happens to me and 90% how I react to it. And so it is with you...we are in charge of our Attitudes.

Charles Swindoll

Let's Define the Term "Educator"

2

"Hello. My name is Miss Ledford and I am the new home economics teacher here at Whiteville High School. I'm new to this area so you will have to help me out for awhile.

"To start with, I graduated from the University of Tennessee at Chattanooga, Magna Cum Laude, with a Bachelor of Science degree in Education with concentration in Vocational Home Economics. I did my student teaching at East Ridge High School and Tyner Middle School, which I'm sure you're all familiar with or have at least heard of. I loved my experiences, so I decided to look for a teaching job straight out of college.

"I was unsuccessful in finding a job my first year, so in order to pay the bills, I worked in jewelry sales for a while and then as a nutritionist. I then had the opportunity to apply for this job and landed a position as a teacher and coach for your school."

As I continued, a hand went up in the air.

"Yes?" I asked.

"Miss Ledford, how old are you?," asked a sly-looking, athletic-type kid from the back of the room, as the rest of his peers laughed and prodded him to ask me more.

"I realize I am very young, twenty-two to be exact, but I do not expect this to be a problem. We can make this thing work if we can get a few things out in the open today."

As the students sat quietly, I continued.

"I sincerely believe this will be, or at least can be, the most successful class you will be a part of this year. I also believe the material for this course is some of the most important information you will need in order to make it in life."

With that part of my introductory remarks given, my students started to look at one another as if to say, "Is this girl for real? Does she really think we expect to learn in this class? Being in this course is just an easy elective. I mean, what could you possibly do to fail a cooking and sewing class ... forget to put on an apron? Burn the bottom of the cookies? Incorrectly stitch a hem?"

It was as if their thoughts were being written on a huge chalkboard at the back of the class. I knew what they were thinking, and I was motivated by it to continue with what I had to say.

"Miss Ledford," called out another student, "Are you married? I mean, is that Miss, Mrs. or Ms.? I was just curious ... I mean, since you're so young ... and it was Chris who wanted to know, anyway." He proudly sank back into his seat, awaiting my answer.

The class went bananas. They had gotten me off the subject and the culprits felt quite proud of themselves that their questions about my personal life had received so much attention from their peers.

"No," I replied. "I am not married, so that officially makes me a *Miss*."

As I was about to finish my statement, another kid with a big grin plastered on his face interrupted to ask, "Do you have a boyfriend? Or does your previous statement mean you're available?"

Ooh's and aah's flew around the room like buzzards around a dead carcass.

"Yes, to answer your question, I do have a boyfriend named Kevin. We have been dating for two years and are very happy. End of discussion. I think you've exhausted my personal life for the first day."

Trying to get the students focused back on why I was there and what I hoped to accomplish was like trying to get a group of four year olds to give up Sesame Street and watch the six o'clock news.

Wow! I didn't realize attention spans were so short and that kids thrived on quizzing teachers about anything and everything but the subject at hand. What a tremendous task to stand before them and, heaven forbid, "lead" them through some sort of educational process.

"This course will consist of a variety of teaching styles and learning techniques. I like to spend time in lectures and note taking, but also a large portion of the class periods will consist of lab work, group activities such as hands-on projects, videos, slideshows and guest speakers. Tests will be given at the end of each unit of study, and will be short answer and essay format. Are there any questions?"

"Miss Ledford," quizzed another anxious student, "I was just wondering ... what kind of car do you drive?"

As laughter circled the room again, I wanted to shout, "That is totally off the subject, you moron. One more off-the-wall question of that nature and I will remove you from the room! Do you understand?"

But I refrained from such a spout of anger and resorted to "What is your name?"

"Greg."

"Thank you. Greg, I happen to drive a Honda Accord SEI sport coupe. It's a dark blue-green color with leather interior and has an awesome Bose sound system!"

"Cool! Sounds really tough. I think we're going to get along pretty good."

As Greg exchanged high fives with his buddies, I contemplated his response. Were they that excited that I drove a "cool," sporty car, or was I going to be bait for the next car theft in the community? Regardless of what they meant, I disregarded thoughts of the latter.

Wondering if my reply was the appropriate way of describing my car, I was reassured by their comments that they liked the idea of a teacher talking their language.

"Moving right along, we have a few more things to cover. I am handing out a packet to each of you that includes a syllabus, classroom policies and procedures, a list of what I expect from you in the areas of attitude and respect, and a complete description of what Vocational Home Economics is all about.

"You need to read this very thoroughly, then put it in a three-ring folder with plenty of ruled notebook paper for the rest of the year. This notebook is a requirement and is expected to be brought to class every day. I will make random folder checks throughout each grading period, so it's crucial to keep up with the folder at all times."

A halfway-frustrated student blurted out, "You mean we actually have to keep up with something? Bring it to class every day? What if I just keep it in my locker, and when you take a folder check I'll go get it. I mean, that's a lot of trouble to keep up with, and besides, I thought this was a cooking class! What good is a folder if you're gonna be cooking?"

"The folder must be with you each day. It is a necessary part of class to record notes given from lectures, keep papers that are handed back to you, and keep up with all handouts and copies I will be giving you on a daily basis.

"And, to answer your other two questions, you will not be allowed to return to your locker and retrieve your notebook if you do not have it with you. Those who are responsible and bring it to class will receive a grade, the rest a zero. Is that understood?

"And lastly, this is not a cooking class! I'm not so sure where you received the information regarding the contents of this course, but you have been most misinformed. Cooking is an integral part of this course, but is only one of the five units of study we will cover. Need I say more?"

The students fell silent and gazed at each other in disbelief and terror. I immediately realized I needed to put my introductory jargon aside and try something that might leave them with a positive view of my course. So, with only ten minutes remaining in the class period, I tried a simple memory game in order to learn their names before they left.

"Let's start with the left side of the room and progress around till I have every name memorized."

"Amy." "Mark." "Sarah." "Tiffany." Each student called out his or her name. When the last name was shouted, I said, "Let's see if I have them all—Amy, Mark, Sarah, Tiffany ... "

I said the names over and over in my mind, and soon knew them all. I said each name and matched each student's face to their given name. Then I repeated the names backwards to check myself one final time.

What a sense of accomplishment to call the kids by their names so quickly! They were truly impressed with this technique, and smiles began to spread across their faces as more names were called.

"One class down, only five more to go!," I reminded myself as the period came to a close. I wished each of my new students a great day and told them I looked forward to seeing them tomorrow.

"I do look forward to seeing them again, don't I?," I wondered as I took a long, deep breath.

I was excited, but somewhat overwhelmed, and I guess I was supposed to be. I was a first-year teacher who had just completed her first full class period, and in my heart I knew I had found my place in this world.

Seeing kids actually take the material I have given them and put it into practice is like nourishment for my soul. It gives me needed energy to try harder each day to make my classes very practical and applicable to life experiences. It shows me the urgency of making each class exciting, so even the most difficult-to-reach student is lured into the activities we are doing.

This challenge alone is one of the unique thrills of being a teacher.

What always moves me is when the kid you never thought you could reach, or the class clown, comes to you and says, "Miss Ledford, this is the best class I've ever taken," or "Miss Ledford, to be a rookie, you sure do know your stuff."

Those words capture my heart for moments in time that will never be forgotten. An occasional remark like this is the reason I continue my journey. This is one of the joys of teaching I couldn't bring to mind many mornings as I drove myself to work.

According to Webster's New World Dictionary, an educator is "one who develops the knowledge, skill, or character of, especially by formal schooling." I perceive this to be about one-quarter of the definition.

After my first-year experience, I do not think it is possible to define the term "educator." Perhaps one could try to find colorful, impressive words that might help us understand what an educator is, but a true and complete explanation is impossible.

Nevertheless, I want to share a few ideas and a partial definition I have come up with over the past few months.

An educator is a lover of people. Be it newborns, toddlers, preschoolers, children, teenagers, young adults, the middle aged or the elderly, educators have a yearning to teach. A genuine love for their audience is a constant, and that love grows stronger with each new experience.

An educator is a motivator of people. Being able to truly motivate a student is like a potter molding the clay for a beautiful, one-of-a-kind piece. It takes lots of shaping and grinding to see the finished product. But, oh, is the final outcome worth it.

Seeing kids motivated and excited lights my fire. The thrill of watching teenagers become involved and confident overwhelms me. It creates in me an unexplainable joy that keeps my gears grinding for yet another day.

Furthermore, educators also have a deep-rooted desire to share their learned knowledge with those around them. The calling is so strong to meet the needs of our young people. There is really no choice in deciding to become an educator—you are destined to be one.

I have found that teaching is much like being a missionary. Missionaries devote their lives to serving God and others and acquire a oneness with the task at hand. They work diligently to see results...results that may not be seen for days, weeks, months, years, or at all. Yet their drive and desire to help and nurture others remains strong enough to keep them involved with their mission.

Being a missionary means volunteering your work, time, skills and energy in exchange for rewards that can't be measured by monetary means—rewards such as seeing a child motivated for the very first time, watching a teenager turn his life around or being involved in helping a family start again by putting the broken pieces together.

These rewards touch the heart in a special way and remind the missionary that quitting is not an option, for many lives are at stake daily.

Because of the stressful lifestyle an educator leads, I have developed a list of 10 simple ideas I feel to be most important in learning to be a successful teacher. They are:

1. A winning attitude. You must believe in yourself. It is vitally important to be your own biggest cheerleader. Work diligently on a daily basis to develop a positive mental attitude.

    Stay informed on everyday issues, read and listen to positive media (such as tapes, motivational seminars, or anything else that might boost your self-esteem). Be active to remain positive; don't sit and stagnate. Overcome the fear of failure. I'm reminded of a saying, "Don't be afraid to go out on a limb. That's where the fruit is."

    And, most importantly, you must be loving and caring. Try to express words of encouragement, and give lots of hugs. It has been said that five billion people go to bed every night hungry for attention. If that's true, we as teachers should try to find more ways for kids to be an active part of our curriculum.

2. Do not let the past control or disturb today; live one day at a time, because today's decisions are tomorrow's realities. Forget the mistakes made yesterday or the things that you "should have" done. Press on!

3. Be content with the circumstances you're in. As a small child, I learned from the Scriptures, "Not that I speak from want; for I have learned to be content in whatever circumstances I am" (Phil. 4:11 NIV).

   I was a first-year teacher. There was nothing I could do to change my situation. I had to endure this new experience and try to learn and grow from my successes and failures. It did not do any good to sit and complain or wish something was different—because it was not.

   Learning to be content in my position at this small country school, in which I was a stranger, was a difficult thing to do. However, only when we accept where we are can we make true progress.

4. Make the "right" choice. Regardless of the situation you might find yourself in, do the right thing. It could be the decision to fail a senior who has taken a course and proven to be lazy, unmotivated, and made very poor grades.

   The student was given the opportunity to do the work, catch up missed assignments, do extra credit, or receive special help, but willingly declined all chances to make a successful venture out of this particular course.

   Graduation time arrives and, if the student fails your course, he or she will not have the required amount of credits to walk with the rest of their class.

   What does a teacher do in times like this? Do you reconsider your decision and give him another chance to pass? As you look back, was there ever a time when his attitude was one of learning and motivation? For some reason or the other did he develop his "I don't care" attitude in the latter stages of the course because he thought his grades were OK? What lifelong effect will this particular incident have on his life?

Most importantly, what is the best and the "right" thing to do for the student?

Wow! What a tough situation to be in. But as the leader in charge, the educator must make the crucial decision.

On the other hand, you could be facing a decision involving a faculty vote. You may be the only one for or against a given situation. Do you have the backbone to stand alone? To give sound reasons to show why you feel this way? Will you be the one to "hang the jury," so to speak?

Educators are put into these precarious situations on a daily basis. However, being able to do this consistently will prove to be rewarding for both you and the system you serve.

5. Motivation. Teachers must have loads of enthusiasm and lots of energy to motivate others. We need to be encouraging others just as they need to be encouraging us. Become a people builder. Give out numerous compliments on any given day to faculty members and students alike.

6. Have a healthy self-image and show confidence. This involves taking good physical care of yourself from day one. Proper diet and adequate exercise along with a good night's sleep (which I was rarely able to get my first year) makes for a healthier you. Learn to view yourself realistically. Boost your self-image by repeating motivational sayings. Dress for success—what you are wearing says something about who you are.

7. Always (or as much as possible) keep a smile on your face. Even when things are not going so well, producing a smile tends to make everything a bit brighter. Usually when you make yourself smile others will find themselves smiling back at you.

8. Do not quit! Never allow self-pity to control. It is so easy to say "That's it!," throw up your hands and give in to the pressure. Don't take the easy way out ... keep on fighting till the end. Quitting should never be a viable choice for a successful educator. Persistence is a quality that's essential in order to stay at this most difficult task of teaching.

9. Do not blame someone else for your problems. There is usually a way out of a less-than-comfortable situation ... blaming someone else for the problem. It's tempting to say, "Well, if so and so had done this or that, we wouldn't be in this predicament anyway!" or "The only reason the fund-raiser failed was because of your attitude toward the whole idea. I can't do it all!"

Don't let yourself get caught in the trap of always finding a scape-goat for the problems that arise. Maybe, just maybe, some of the blame belongs on you. If so, analyze the problem and look for positive solutions.

10. Finally, remember that there is hope for enduring your situation— something good does come out of this. The rewards are great for an educator. Even after countless hours of giving, giving, and more giving, the educator receives some valuable gifts in return for his or her hard work and dedication.

A hundred years from now
It will not matter
What my bank account was,
The sort of house I lived in
Or the kind of clothes I wore.
But the world may be different
Because I was important
In the life of a child.

The Costs of Being an Educator

3

"HOTDOGS! NACHOS! ANYWAY YOU LIKE 'EM ... HOTDOGS! NACHOS! ONE DOLLAR!" were the often-heard chants echoing from our concession stand on any given fall evening during home football games. What seemed like an eternal afternoon of opening up gigantic cans of chili and spicy nacho cheese sauce we had purchased at the local warehouse was now a fading memory, as hungry fans began to line up for tonight's "dinner."

"I'll take three hotdogs, one all the way, one with mustard and ketchup only, one with mayonnaise ... you do have mayo, don't ya? And could you put just a bit of that cheese sauce on top? And the other plain, no ... could you just put a little dab of chili on that, please? And a few onions."

"Is that all, sir?"

"Ah, what the heck! Give me an order of nachos and three Cokes."

"We don't have Cokes, sir. You will have to purchase the Cokes over to the left at the other concession stand."

"Why do you have to wait in two lines just to get something to eat? This is ridiculous! Just cancel my order and I'll get a hotdog over there."

"Sir, the concessions are divided up by school clubs. The other stand only serves candy, beverages, popcorn and gum. Would you still like to get the hotdogs and nachos?"

"Yea. Just give 'em to me ... I'm starved to death and I'm in a hurry ... it's kick-off time!"

"That will be four dollars ... Thank you."

Who did this guy think he was? Who did he think we were? A full-service, four-star, top-of-the-line concession stand with plenty of paid workers to meet the needs of every angry, hungry or impatient customer that comes along? You've got to be kidding.

Realizing that it was 35 degrees with a five-to-ten mile-per-hour wind whirling in and out of this portable concession stand made matters even worse. What could be more exciting than to spend your Friday night selling hotdogs and nachos to a bunch of cold, hungry people?

My hands began to get numb. I wondered if I could wrap another hotdog or make one more trip to the other concession stand. I had been using their microwave to rewarm cheese and chili that had gotten cold, because overloaded circuits from both concessions were causing power failures about every twenty minutes. Just as the hotdogs were beginning to boil steadily, the power would go off for ten to fifteen minutes. This battle with on-again, off-again electricity was just an added nuisance to contend with.

Nevertheless, I had three or four faithful, dedicated students who volunteered to help prepare and sell food at each game. The enthusiasm from these kids seemed to make the time pass a little faster. They enjoyed greeting, serving, and collecting money from friends and family members.

This was a chance for them to display some leadership responsibilities and they did a good job. However, the bulk of the errand running was left up to me.

Most of the kids couldn't stay after school because they had to get rides home or deal with their parents' work schedules. They would return to the ballfield early, but I was forced to run around like a chicken with its head cut off in order to get chili in crock pots, nachos in containers, carry boxes of chips down from the home economics department, run extension cords to the other concession stand's power supply, get the money box from the secretary, wipe down the food service area, and on, and on, and on!

"What am I doing here?," I would exclaim as I cranked open another can of chili. "Why is this required of me? This is slave labor!"

Why was I never told that being a home economics teacher required operating a concession stand in near-freezing temperatures till all hours of the night in order to make a few dollars for our Future Homemakers of

America club? Why did veteran teachers not warn me that teaching involved so many different aspects? This was never discussed in any of my college "education methods" courses.

All in all, we made two to three hundred dollars for our efforts throughout the football season. This probably comes to about one dollar an hour when you consider all the hours spent on planning, shopping, preparing, selling and clean-up. We quickly realized that this method of fund-raising was not cost-effective. The profits received were not a great enough reward for our efforts.

Looking back on this whole ordeal, I would do things quite differently if given that option. "There must be a better way to make money than this," I thought. Regardless of what my principal thought would be the best way for our club to raise funds, I had an even better idea: I would gladly donate the two hundred dollars next year. After all, when I considered my time, gas, energy, and doctor bills (I spent two Saturday mornings at the doctor's office with a cold, a sore throat and congestion), I could actually make money. On top of it all, I could look forward next year to purchasing a hotdog as a hungry fan, eagerly anticipating the kick-off.

During my college years, I remember quizzing several of my peers who were working toward being "teachers of the future." Some of the questions I wanted answers to were, "What are the costs of being an educator? What is actually involved in this whole teacher idea? What is it really like out there in the schools? Is college preparing me for what lies ahead?"

After careful analysis of my first-year teaching experience, I have found the following to be true: Only 110 percent of a person's mind, soul, heart and being is required to be a teacher. It only costs a lifetime of giving, preparing, planning, organizing and implementing various strategies. It's always thinking ahead, missing many hours of good, solid sleep, trying to conjure up a new way to approach a concept or an innovative way to tackle an objective that keeps educators burning the midnight oil.

And speaking of burning the midnight oil, no one bothered to tell me that this wonderful career, which was going to give me more free time than I'd know what to do with, was going to occupy my mind twenty-four hours a day, night after night after night.

Then I began to wonder if I was the only one experiencing all this turmoil, so I began to question colleagues and coworkers—only to find they were dealing with much the same problems as I was.

Being totally consumed with the functions and operations of my school was not really a choice—it went along with the job. But waking up at 3:00 a.m. just to jot down a note to myself about school so I wouldn't forget it by morning was going a bit far, I thought. Dreaming quite often of events of the previous day or of events that were coming up on my agenda seemed to be a bit much. Suddenly, my life was saturated with this whole teaching lifestyle, and it had entrapped me to the point that I was unsure I wanted to stay around to enjoy the rest.

Nevertheless, time moved on. I began to sleep in increments of two to three hours before being awakened by the heaviness of the day weighing on my heart.

I thought if I could just get a five-hour block of sleep, I would wake up ready to conquer the world. I would have enough energy to transform my teaching into a motivating, powerful, arena in which kids would be moved and stirred like never before.

If only my energy level could be higher and my enthusiasm could last until the final bell of just one day, oh, what a difference I could make.

Restless nights were the result of my not being able to put an end to the day, to say to myself, "It's over. What's done is done. Goodnight. Start over tomorrow—it will be a whole new day."

Having the ability to finalize things and move forward is something I have had trouble with. I always want to say, "If only I would have ... ," or "Maybe if I had handled that differently," or "If given the opportunity to respeak those words or take back a harsh word spoken in a stressful situation, I would ... if only, if only!"

I soon learned you cannot do this. This type of behavior is self-destructive. It keeps your morale low, and self-esteem levels are dampened, sometimes even resulting in paranoia.

On the contrary, this constant self-evaluation and self-analysis can be positive. My desire to reach a professional level as an educator is helped by the methods I use for personal renewal.

Being a perfectionist is something of a self-checking system. I tend to be much more organized, sticking to a tight schedule of events and receiving strong satisfaction when a task is completed.

Now let's take a closer look at the big picture. What does an educator actually have to do to be good? What is sacrificed in order to become a renowned teacher? I asked all these questions and more, and here are a few answers I found.

First of all, as with any other professional career, college costs are extremely high. The financial burden that most would-be teachers take on is incredible.

Most students take out loans to put themselves through college. Others work their way through. Some get government grants for assistance, and a few lucky individuals receive scholarships. The other small percentage are blessed to have a family sending them to college. Thankfully, I was in the latter category.

However the college degree is financed, the salaries that await educators are lower than those in other professional fields. This alone can be frustrating for the beginning teacher. Somehow, growing up and throughout the college experience, I failed to realize how low the salaries are in education.

Secondly, an educator must dedicate countless hours to his or her work. Because of this, other things such as your social life must be put on hold. The main drive and focus is school life, and everything else revolves around it.

What could be so difficult about a "cushy" 8:00 a.m. to 3:00 p.m. teaching job? Society has labeled educators as having these absurd working hours, which is one of the biggest myths educators must continually knock down. I was quite surprised to discover the true workday of a teacher.

During my first year, I was determined to "beat the system," work hard all day and leave at 3:00. Somehow this didn't work. It never mattered that I stayed up until early morning to grade papers, plan lessons and organize in order to be ahead the next day.

Tomorrow always brought a new life of its own. Even coming in early the next morning was not the answer, so I began to stay late. I found myself staying until 4:00 or 4:15 so I could get at least some of my work done.

Every school is a unique entity, and most require much more than teaching. Extracurricular activities are a topic that always comes up during the initial interview.

"In what area are you most suited to help us in extracurricular events?" I was asked. At this point, you must be ready to choose something or something will be chosen for you.

I haven't really figured this mystery out, but principals say I "look like" a cheerleading sponsor. That I am not! How does a person look to be eligible for that job? Green, I asked? Wet behind the ears? With no disrespect toward cheerleaders, this is a job for someone else. I was a cheerleader in my elementary school days and heaven forbid I should "look" as though I could handle a group of these cheering girls.

I am somehow able to move past the cheerleading sponsor idea.

"So, what would you possibly be interested in?," he continued. "Faculty members are strongly encouraged to participate and be an integral part of the students' extracurricular activities."

"Basketball! I would like to coach girls high school basketball!" I insisted. There was a long pause. I felt the silence. Did I not look like a basketball coach?

After several minutes of talking through the idea, it became a possibility. I had the opportunity to become the girls' assistant basketball coach if the head coach agreed. What seemed to be only a dream a few minutes earlier was now a distinct possibility. The meeting with the coach would be the deciding factor.

That coaching job did, in fact, come to me. Now my days would end even later than before. Practices, games, summer camps and meetings. The whole idea overwhelmed me. Days and nights would begin to mesh. I tried to remember what I thought teaching was going to be like. For some reason, the answer never came to me.

I cannot possibly relate how my life changed during this "rookie" year. Why couldn't someone have warned me? Why was I never told that teaching required so much in the physical, emotional, social and psychological areas?

I wish the reality of the lifestyle had presented itself earlier to me. If only ...

One of the questions I'm often asked is, "Why does a person want to teach? What is it that drives a being to eat, sleep, and drink school life?"

I was sitting in my apartment one evening doing some casual writing when a distinct analogy entered my mind. As I thought through the idea, it became a vivid picture of the education process. It painted a portrait I could identify with.

Since the presidential campaign began, I had spent a great deal of time analyzing the campaign process. The enormous amounts of money spent on advertisements amazed me. Millions of dollars, months of "selling yourself," and various other preparations had to be made to compete for the title of President of the United States.

A lifetime of vested political interests, holding significant offices and networking was needed to win the majority vote. A proven, responsible background had to be intact for the American public to endorse your efforts toward the highest office in our country.

All of this for approximately $200,000 a year? Other perks come along which would greatly increase the actual dollar amount, but my point is this: why would a person engage himself in such an awesome task? Why do individuals, year after year, decide to take on the hectic campaign process and strive to be elected?

The answer is very simple. For reasons other than money. Reasons such as the power that comes with being the President of the United States, the personal rewards, the need to satisfy the longing to achieve, and the desire to help people make a better world for themselves.

All of these reasons are directly tied to those of a teacher. Teaching is a political occupation in itself. School systems operate much like political structures.

As a new teacher fresh out of college, it is difficult to land a full-time job. You begin to advertise and "sell yourself" by shipping out cover letters and resume packets, making phone calls, interviewing and networking among existing educators. More money is invested and time is expended in hopes of getting hired. Unfortunately, jobs are usually attained by "who you know" rather than "what you know."

The political game continues and you finally get a teaching position. It may take a year, two, or even three years for it to happen, but eventually the job will come if you can outlast your opponents. At this time you may find yourself exclaiming, "I did all of this politicking and fighting for this?" But you can be encouraged by the words of Aristotle, "The roots of education are bitter, but the fruit is sweet."

An educator fights his or her way into the system for the rewards involved in teaching young people—to see children grow and learn before their very eyes. Personal satisfaction comes in knowing that you are making a difference in someone else's life. Building the respect of the students and living a positive example are two things that most educators strive for. And, in most cases, I believe that teachers enjoy the sense of power and authority that comes with the job.

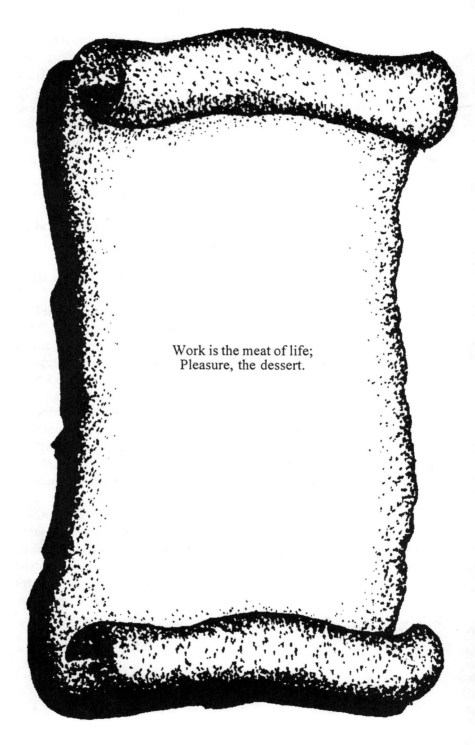

Work is the meat of life;
Pleasure, the dessert.

Me? ...Have a Social Life?

4

It was 12:05 a.m. and I was pondering the menu at Waffle House. "Can I stomach a chef salad at this time of the night?" I asked myself for the third night in a row. "What about a BLT? Or maybe I could just settle for a nice hot waffle and some crisp bacon with orange juice." Noticing the time, the latter would be more appropriate. "I could grab another moment's sleep and skip breakfast," I thought.

Trying to relax, but muddling through various aspects of our basketball team's just-completed victory over a rival school, I wondered, "What am I doing here? It's only five hours till the alarm will sound and I'm sitting here listening to Billy Ray Cyrus sing 'Achy Breaky Heart,' waiting for a bite to eat."

As I waited to be served, I watched several unusual characters go in and out. Mostly they were young "kooks" with green and red hair, combat clothes, pierced everything, smoking anything, and I wondered, "Is this the generation we are raising?"

When my food finally arrived, I said a little prayer and quickly inhaled it. Kevin ordered an apple pie for dessert just to extend our "date" a few minutes longer.

It was now 12:59 a.m. and out the door we went, realizing that, at best, I would be asleep by 2:00 a.m., after I was able to take care of a few necessities at the apartment and organize my things for the next day.

Upon arriving home, I picked up my mail and hurriedly went inside, to be greeted by an answering machine that resembled a blinking Christmas tree. One, two, three, four, five, six calls to possibly return. Rewind. Stop. Play.

Message 1: "Jada, this is Mom. Please give me a call when you get in. Love you. Bye."

"One down, only five to go," I thought.

Message 2: "Hello, Miss Ledford. This is the dry cleaners. I was just calling to tell you that your black jeweled applique blazer was damaged in the cleaning process. We do apologize for the inconvenience."

Apologize? My $150 favorite, one-of-kind blazer is damaged and they apologize? I'm a teacher, you know. It's not like I have money to burn ... my blazer?

I took a deep breath and somehow focused my thoughts on the next evening. Every night this week had been filled with either a game or a practice, so I was hoping for a time of rest and a time to catch up.

"No more late-night Waffle House visits for at least one night," I thought. "Only peace and quiet, an evening nap on my cozy little couch, and a good book to top it off."

Message 3: "Jada, this is Mom. Don't worry about calling me back. I just wanted to let you know I'll be down to spend the night tomorrow. See you about 4:00 p.m. Love you. Bye."

What? Tomorrow? Anytime in the next 365 days, but not tomorrow! I panicked. I must call her back ... No! I can't. Oh my gosh ... it's 1:37 a.m.

Message 4: "Miss Ledford ... this is Mrs. Grace Jones from the Chattanooga Area Home Economics Association, and I just wanted to remind you of our association meeting tomorrow night at 6:00 p.m. It will be held at the Agricultural Extension Office and the theme will be 'Homemade Preparations for the Holidays' ... look forward to seeing you there."

"Oh! I completely forgot about the meeting. I would love to attend and visit with everyone. I can't go. Mom is coming down ... No she isn't! What will I do?"

Message 5: "Hey Jada, this is John ... Where the heck are you? Man, I really need to talk to you about something very important. Call me back whenever you get in. Please call me tonight. I'll be up. See ya!"

It's 1:45 a.m., which means 12:45 for him in the Central Time Zone. I had better give him a quick call. A quick call ... I never talk to my brother for less than an hour. I'm exhausted. I've got to get in bed.

Message 6: "Jada, this is Sharon in the office. Just wanted to make sure you received your notice of the water being turned off throughout the complex on Thursday, December 15th, from 6:00 a.m. to 2:00 p.m. We have a water pipe problem which must receive immediate attention. Thanks. Talk to you later."

NO WATER TOMORROW? I must shower tonight? Maybe I'll fall asleep in the process and never wake up again, I thought.

This was just more than I could handle. I could not continue to live this way! I would not! I could not do it one day longer! I was sleepy and tired ... I had to have a break!

Kevin quickly realized the best thing for him to do would be to slip out before I totally lost it. He did not like to see me when I reached this point. He felt totally helpless. He wished me a good night's sleep, gave me a kiss, and left.

I settled down some and quickly jumped in the shower. When will this end? Will I ever live a normal life again? Have I ever lived a normal life? And now that I think about it, what is a normal life?

Anyway, I threw a big pity-party. My morale had hit an all-time low. I felt depressed and trapped. I had no outlets. No time for myself or Kevin. My social life was beginning to resemble that of a slowly dying flower. What was once beautiful, full of color and texture, so exciting as to make everyone around take notice, was now wilting away. I was becoming a bit droopy, almost lifeless, and I wanted my circumstances to change.

Teaching requires every ounce of your being at all times. The tremendous stress of putting in so many hours becomes overwhelming.

Coaching occupied one of the largest parts of my life. I was coaching or attending two to three games a week and getting home around 11:00 p.m., which made for a fifteen- to eighteen-hour workday. Not only was I the assistant girls' basketball coach, but I was teaching five different subjects each day, which required an extended amount of lesson preparation. This created an undue amount of pressure and stress that was mounting up to the point where I was neglecting myself.

While most of my friends would enjoy an evening out for dinner, going to the movies or shopping, I was slaving over lab projects that had to be graded by the next morning. My friends stopped asking me to join them after they realized my answer was always no, along with some long, drawn-out explanation of why I could not go.

This new stress of putting in so many hours was something I had not anticipated. I thought teachers had fun ... and something of an easy job. I had been programmed from childhood that teaching was the ideal profession for a mother, since she would have summers off with the kids and would be home to share in the special holidays throughout the year. So surely I must be lucky to be a part of this profession as a single person.

I didn't feel lucky. I did not have a moment to myself. And I was neglecting my own needs (not wants, but needs). My stress level was at an all-time high and there was no slowing down in sight. We were in the middle of basketball season and I was running a tighter ship than ever.

Not only was my teaching putting excessive time constraints on me, but I was coming home to another full-time job. This "second job," as I call it, included cleaning, cooking, grocery buying, washing clothes, paying bills, etc., and, for some, caring for children is thrown on top of all this. No wonder teacher burnout happens so often. This type of lifestyle is like a ticking bomb ... with an explosion seconds away, and destruction inevitable. At this point, I just needed to "blow the whistle" and call a "time-out."

Looking at my daily schedule, I wondered where I could drop an activity and give myself a break. As I looked over my options, there were a few things I realized.

First of all, I lived in the Eastern Time Zone and worked in the Central Time Zone. This was a nuisance that worked both for and against my schedule. In the morning, I could sleep a bit later, but in the evenings, it was a tremendous loss to see that extra hour disappear as I crossed Rock Creek Mountain. This alone put me way behind schedule and made for an extra-long day.

Secondly, my family began to see less, much less, of me after I accepted this new job as a teacher. Since all of my family lived out of town, spending time together became a real scheduling problem. My mom and dad lived only one hour away, yet I was seeing them just once a month, on the average. My parents began to come to my basketball games when it was convenient, just to get, as my dad would say, "a glimpse of his daughter." Of course, no meaningful communication could take place at the games because of my responsibilities.

As far as seeing my brother, my one and only sibling who lived in Nashville, Tennessee just three hours away, visits were few and far between. The best opportunity I had to meet him was during my required, summer vocational conference in Murfreesboro. This idea of dovetailing work and family life was a relatively new idea I was not sure I liked.

Third, my dating life was suffering. I was in a steady relationship with my boyfriend, Kevin. Our dates consisted of being at the computer until all hours of the morning typing tests, creating new worksheets and projects and averaging grades.

If we were not pounding away at the keyboard, we were probably at the supermarket retrieving groceries for the following day of home economics food labs. Or we might be scampering through area retail stores trying to round up supplies for an upcoming club event, or eating a late-night Waffle House entrée.

Regardless of what was on the agenda for the evening or the weekend, Kevin never failed to stay by my side, supporting me in a professional and personal manner I had never been exposed to before. This much-needed encouragement was one of the biggest reasons I could continue with this schedule at the level I did.

Lastly, my church participation and acceptance of leadership roles there began to dwindle. Even with early dismissal from basketball practice on Wednesday night, I still couldn't make it to church due to the time change.

When you become so involved with a school, especially when you're also a coach, there comes a real struggle with your allegiance to so many groups of kids. People at church on Sundays often asked me, "Jada, would you be interested in teaching a Sunday evening course for our youth on topics in today's society that are plaguing them?" or "Would you go on a rotating system of teaching a youth Bible study?" or "Would you consider taking a Sunday school class next year?"

What a difficult thing to say no to. There were so many opportunities in the church, but I was teaching each and every day, six full classes (approximately 140 teenagers), and then leaving to spend another two to four hours with my girls on the basketball team. It is hard to spend a sixth day in the same role as a teacher in the church.

Nevertheless, I did take on some of those short-term teaching responsibilities, only to feel at times that maybe I needed to be the student in some area of my life. Church life was something I felt very strongly about, and it was a place where I needed to be the learner instead of the teacher.

I know making this type of decision does not come easily for anyone. Teachers are not the only ones who go through these struggles.

Any person—be he a professional, blue collar worker, homemaker, college or technical student—must juggle the various roles that come along in this wonderful society in which we live. Each person must find his or her niche and then work like crazy not only to occupy that spot, but to make life more beautiful and productive for themselves, and for those around them.

With this comes a responsibility to be accountable for what we produce, or cause to be produced. And in my short time here on Earth, I have found this to be an awesome task.

Reprinted with permission from Bruce Plante.

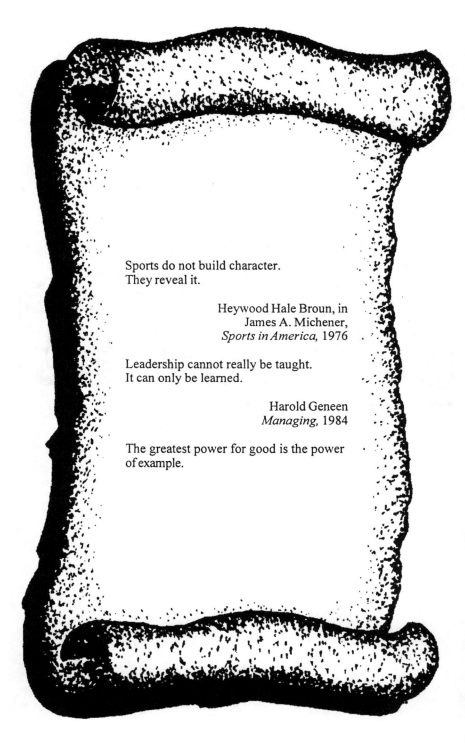

Sports do not build character.
They reveal it.

> Heywood Hale Broun, in
> James A. Michener,
> *Sports in America,* 1976

Leadership cannot really be taught.
It can only be learned.

> Harold Geneen
> *Managing,* 1984

The greatest power for good is the power
of example.

The Power of Coaching

5

Rushing home from church with great anticipation about meeting my new basketball team, I became a bit nervous. As I began to think through this first meeting with these high school girls, my mind began to wonder, "Will they accept me on first impression, or will they play 'hard to get' and feel me out over an extended period of time, making me wait for their approval or disapproval?"

This initial meeting was like going to that first job interview—all the anxiety and uncertainty was overwhelming. It was a difficult time to present an "at ease" aura.

I felt almost sick inside. "What a big opportunity to be an assistant high school girls' basketball coach on my first teaching job," I thought as I drove toward the gymnasium.

As I walked in wearing my basketball attire of sweatshorts, a T-shirt and Reeboks, I felt my heart beat at a faster pace. Suddenly my mouth was dry and my confidence level plummeted. Was I letting a group of high school girls intimidate me?

As I walked into the lobby, I saw the entrance to the gym and the familiar sights, sounds and smells from my high school days: the squeaking of tennis shoes on the court, whistles blowing, coaches yelling and giving instructions from the sidelines, and the sweaty aroma of hard-working athletes.

I began to daydream about my high school years—no responsibility, a care-free lifestyle, and all the memories of previous basketball camps, especially my ninth grade camp initiation, when I awoke to a mixture of bran cereal, baby oil, lotion, peanut butter, jelly and shaving cream matted in my hair; brushing my teeth with a toothbrush saturated in baby oil; and quacking like a duck down the halls blindfolded. I was being made to do things in front of an audience of coaches and other players that I won't get too specific about.

I felt I was going back in time, or maybe even longing to relive that period of my life. But whatever was happening was making me feel emotions I hadn't felt in quite some time.

As I jolted myself out of this dreamy state, I went toward the bleachers and passed a group of girls whose attention was frozen on a basketball game. I said a few "excuse me's" and found a seat, only to notice I was getting some pretty strong looks from these girls.

"Could that possibly be my girls?" I thought as I scanned the gym in search of the head coach. "There he is, down on the floor ... his team is playing, and, oh my gosh, that is his team ... I mean our team."

As I made eye contact with some of the girls, I wasn't sure this was going to work. I was not feeling accepted and I hadn't even met them yet.

Whispers were exchanged down the bench and attention began to shift from the game to me, the new mystery coach. Comments were flying and I just sat there, wondering what was being said.

I was very uneasy by the time I met the girls after the game.

"Girls, this is Coach Ledford," explained a proud Coach Barkley.

"She will be the new assistant coach and will prove to be a big help to us this year." He continued with a very genial introduction before allowing me to say a few words.

To be honest, I have absolutely no idea what I said to those girls. It is all one big blur. But whatever I said must have worked, because that was the beginning of one of the most beautiful relationships I have ever experienced.

"Hey, Coach Ledford!," "O.K., Coach!," "I don't understand, Coach!," were just three of the clichés I heard in my new role as a coach.

I never realized the incredible responsibility that would come along with the title "Coach." Almost instantly my life changed, as I began to build special relationships with my new team. I realized right away that this meant giving another piece of my life and heart to my profession.

The camaraderie that develops is awesome. Cookouts, swimming parties, Christmas and holiday outings began to be a large part of my social life so I could get to know my players.

We grew very close to each other in a short amount of time. Bonds formed and these were "my girls." And in my mind, I was the legendary "Coach Ledford."

One of my most alarming realizations was discovering the power of coaching. People look at you through different eyes. The entire community, parents, other teachers, students, and players expect the coach to know how to win! Someone once said, "Winning isn't everything, but losing is!"

That sums it up.

I have found there are basically two types of people who coach. Winners and losers. A winner is a coach with drive and force. He or she is determined to put in the necessary preparation to see success as an end result. A winner tends to glow. He or she is always ready to chat about the team, player talent, potential for the coming season or anything else team-related.

This type of coach takes on a sense of team ownership. Authority issues are rarely a problem, due to the understanding that exists between the players and coach.

On the other hand, some coaches are losers. Losers have a nonchalant attitude for the game. The only reason they coach is to hang out with their buddies that are coaches, or because no one else would take the job. When asked about their team, they try to change the subject, joke about the coming year, or comment "beats flippin' burgers as a second job."

Losers are wasting their time. They are setting a poor example for eager kids who want to play the game. Losers don't work very hard because they're not driven to see a successful outcome. "You win some, you lose some" is something a loser would say.

Losers are everywhere. Winners are not. A winner's thrust is his or her positive actions and reactions to those around.

Why have I said all of this? To make a clear point about being a leader. Leadership is the most important quality needed to be a successful coach.

I have found that kids do what is expected of them. Only a true leader can enforce guidelines and get results. Parents often have a hard time agreeing with me on this point. They say, "Come on over to my house and expect my kids to clean their room. Then you'll see your theory trashed."

But my reply is quite simple. The enforcement has to be consistent. What type of negative consequences do your children face if they choose not to clean their rooms? Sophocles said, "What you cannot enforce, do not command."

The same goes in coaching. This basic principle applies to every aspect of life, be it raising children, coaching, teaching or managing employees on the job. The leader is the link that keeps the chain in one piece.

So what are the characteristics of a good leader? Here are some qualities every true leader must possess:

1. A leader must be able to take criticism. No person in a position of authority is insulated from it. One must learn to sort out the constructive criticism, from which one can learn, and the malicious, which one must ignore.

2. A leader must learn to stand adversity. Things will not always go well. Failures will happen. A good leader will bounce back.

3. A leader must be able to delegate authority. He must be able to give up power, to trust those under him.

4. A leader must make decisions. The person who cannot take a stand does not deserve to lead others.

5. A leader must be free from prejudices. Someone once said that prejudice is a luxury "only little people can afford."

6. A leader must learn to praise others, to share credit, and to give credit where it is due. If he tries to take credit for everything, he will only frustrate those under him.

7. A leader must be able to concentrate under difficult conditions, to keep the goal constantly in mind, to keep his or her head when all about are losing theirs.

8. A true leader will assume responsibility for his or her own mistakes.

9. A leader will not try to avoid responsibility for the mistakes of others.

10. A good leader will grow and learn. Stagnation is not leadership. (*Bits and Pieces*, 1986)

How does a coach enforce the rules? Strong discipline? Rewards for following standards?

Answer: by setting the proper example. The coach must be the leader in charge at all times. For instance, on my team we have few rules. These are clearly explained at the start of the season and discussed from time to time.

If a player is caught breaking a rule, there are consequences. Everyone is fully aware of the guidelines and consents to upholding the rules while being a part of the team.

But from time to time, we have a situation where rules are broken, and it's crucial for the coach to enforce the consequences at this time. The rest of the team wants to see if the rules are really valid. Coaching isn't always easy, and this is a good example of when it gets hairy. Confrontations with players and parents are never enjoyable, but a necessary part of the job.

To give you a clear picture of what I'm really talking about, let me share a situation that occurred during my first year as an assistant coach at this small, country school.

A game against another well-known county high school was to be played on Friday night. We (the head coach and I) tried to get the girls "hyped up" for the game, reminding them of how hard they had worked and all the long hours spent on practice. This was, we told them, the game to pull it all together and make it come alive.

Realizing that we had been beaten by the other team at their gym only weeks earlier in a very close game, the girls seemed a bit intimidated. Our rivals had a big girl inside who carried the team in scoring, and in no way did our post players match up to her in height. But we were going to give them a fight till the end, win or lose.

Friday finally came after a tough week of district play. To be quite honest, Coach Barkley and I were disappointed with the effort we were getting from our team. I was doing motivational talks, seemingly to no avail.

The girls were tired and we knew it. We were playing, on the average, three games a week and that was wearing us down. Putting that behind us, our eyes were focused on the game, and what a biggie it was going to be.

Our gymnasium was usually only 30 to 40 percent full, but we had drawn a tremendous crowd, with a number of students who generally did not come out to support basketball making a special effort to attend. This would be a very tough and emotional game, and the community wanted to be there to see it "live."

As our girls began their warm-up drills, I could feel the anxiety. I was more wired than I was during my coaching debut. I was pumped and I think everyone knew it. Our girls were going to win, I just knew it in my heart, and I could not wait for the victory.

As we watched the girls, I noticed some of the starters were not shooting well. They were joking, laughing, and sort of goofing off. I yelled, "Girls! Get serious. Stay focused. Pull that elbow in, Melissa. Pivot the other way, Cindy. Jump and then shoot, Kim—you're gonna eat the ball if you release on the way up."

Their nonchalance disturbed me, and I was wondering if Coach Barkley was seeing the same thing.

We retreated to the dressing room for our final few words with the team. As we all sat down, Coach Barkley began going over various plays and special situations.

"Do you know where you're supposed to be, Kim, when we run "Box X" or "Stack Cross?" What about the press? Angela, if we get a girl in foul trouble, are you focused enough to remember the plays and what you're supposed to do?"

After these questions came a flood of panic-stricken comments.

"Coach, do I do this? Where am I supposed to be if the ball goes to the other side? What if they switch to a zone defense?"

The team acted as if we had never been over the details of the plays before, and here we were with only a couple of minutes left till we played our biggest rival of the year, a must-win game, and we were caught up in a question-and-answer session.

Regardless of their reasons for being so unsure about the game, whether nervousness, tiredness, or just plain forgetfulness, Coach Barkley had had about all he could take. He slammed his clipboard on the floor and said, "Coach Ledford, see if you can do anything with them. I've done all I can do and it just does not seem to be working. I'm through. I'm outta here—bring them out in a few minutes."

Our calm, even-tempered head coach, with twenty-three years of experience, had just walked out on this young bunch of bug-eyed girls and left them to a first-year teacher and coach who was scared to death. In my mind I was saying, "This is not really happening ... it can't be ... wipe all this away and motivate the girls ... fire them up ... that's all you can do at this point."

Just as the door slammed shut, I began a mini-sermon on the importance of staying focused: during practice, so you will understand and learn the plays; during off time, so you can review and practice on your weaknesses at home; and at game time, so you can easily recall all that has been learned.

I exclaimed, "We want to see players who can put it all together, and at this point, we're wondering if we have any of those on our team. You've gotta want to win—losing is not a choice. If you think you're gonna lose, then you've already lost before the game starts. Think positive. Encourage one another. Become absorbed with the game and learn even while you are on the bench."

As the girls came to their feet they seemed to be a bit more motivated, or at least I was. I gave them one last challenge—to show us what they were made of—we said our team prayer, chant, and out the door we went. As the girls filed out of the locker room, we passed Coach Barkley in the corridor.

"Well, Coach, who's the starting five?" I asked with much anticipation and curiosity. With a shrug of his shoulders that indicated he still did not know, and a look that said he was at a loss for words, he pointed me in the direction of the scorer's table.

"You decide. You choose the line-up ... do what you think is best. I've tried various approaches and I want to see what you think."

Me? Pick the starting line-up? I'd never done this before. Why couldn't it be another game—not the county rival of the year? What if I make a mistake? What are the parents, and the players, going to think of my decision?

As all these thoughts raced through my mind, I slowly walked to the scorekeeper and made my selections. As he checked off the girls' numbers, I could feel the audience close in on me. But I felt good about my "going against the odds" decision. It couldn't hurt and it might even help, I reasoned.

Turning away from the table, Coach Barkley and I made eye contact. "So what's it gonna be?"

"You're not going to believe this, and I'm not even sure you'll agree, but here it is: Keri, Angela, Cindy, Dawn and Lisa. I feel these girls need a chance. Keri, Angela and Lisa haven't started a game this year, but they have continued to be strong, supportive teammates.

"This switch-up may be really good for us; I think it will confuse the other coach. He'll wonder what's going on. Furthermore, putting three of our best players on the bench may be good for them. They need to realize the team can exist without them. Their work ethic has slackened ... let's let them sit and think about how much they really want to be out on the court. This will also give them a chance to support their teammates from the bench, a view I'm sure they're unfamiliar with. So what do you think?"

"I say go with it. We'll see what happens."

As the buzzer sounded, it was time to huddle up and prepare for the game.

The announcer introduced the visiting team first, with their usual players heading the lineup. When their big girl, who consistently led their team in scoring, gave high fives to her teammates, I could see a look of dismay come across our starting center's face. Thinking she would jump against her on the tip-off and match up with her one-on-one was unnerving her.

I wondered how she would feel if she knew the night's lineup.

"And now, your Whiteville Lady Tiger's starting lineup will be ... Number 14, Keri Baxter!"

With that introduction, it was as if the noisy, pumped-up audience had seen a ghost. Someone even had to nudge Keri and say, "Run on out to the center of the court, you're starting!," since she also was taken by surprise.

"Number 20, Angela Wells!"

As a few more disturbed claps came from the audience, heads began to go back and forth. The bedazzled crowd of supporters whispered as if to ask, "What is that coaching crew up to? What are they trying to pull? Have they really lost their minds?"

As the third number was called, "Number 24, Lisa Johnson!," it was obvious some of the fans were truly baffled, and, deep down, I loved it.

"Number 12, Dawn Allen, and Number 10, Cindyyyyyyy Burgess."

Whew! It's over for now, I thought. But this was only the beginning of what was in store for me.

As the game got under way, the opposing team jumped out to a quick lead. We had several early turnovers that got us off to a slow start. As much as it looked like I had made a big mistake, I chose to leave the same girls in the game.

"Work hard, Keri, you can do it," I screamed from the bench. "Watch her from behind, Angela. Guard the ball. Move girls, move. You have to want the ball. Watch your passes. Lob the ball, Keri, she's a lot taller than most post girls. Come on. You can do it!"

I was still convinced my strategy was going to prove successful, but I will admit there were times I felt very uncomfortable.

This was a real learning experience for our entire team. As I glanced down the bench, I noticed that Coach Barkley was his usual self, offering a word or two every now and then. I remember, after getting eight points behind, looking down at him and saying, "I'm gonna leave them in, coach ... they're gonna have to score two straight times on the same girl for me to pull her."

With a halfway nod of agreement, we readjusted our thoughts to the game.

I motioned to Cindy to call a timeout, mainly to give these girls a minute to breathe. Some of them hadn't seen this much playing time all season, and I did not want to lose anyone to heat exhaustion or dehydration.

As we began to offer words of encouragement, I reminded them of positions for certain plays. You could feel the audience expecting some substitutions. After we huddled together and chanted "Go Team," I sent the starting five back in the game.

From this point until halftime, I began to notice some less-than-desirable things about our bench. One kid, in particular, was having a more-than-difficult time adjusting to this new role as "bench warmer."

It was very uncomfortable and somewhat degrading for her, as was obvious by the look on her face and her dampened enthusiasm. The usual intensity in her eyes had diminished as she sat and watched her teammates play the entire half.

Despite eleven unanswered first half points by the Lady Warriors' post girl, our team outscored them 28-21 in the half. We entered the locker room, seemingly on our way to victory, and I was soaring like an eagle. My adrenaline level had hit an all-time high, and this was a feeling I hoped would linger for the rest of the night.

If only you could have been there to see the excitement from this group of girls! As some of you have experienced firsthand through coaching, there is no greater feeling than to take a risk and see a successful outcome.

After a brief period of congratulations for a job well done, I reminded them that this was only the first half.

"We are halfway there, girls. We came in as underdogs and knew we had our work cut out for us, but we have proved to ourselves and to the community that we can match up to anyone, and we will fight hard to the end.

"Please remember, we're not expected to win. No one sitting in the stands expects you to win, so there is no pressure at all ... none! We want to continue what we've been doing: work the ball and look for Dawn inside. If she's tied up, take the open outside shot, or fake and drive to the basket for the foul. Keep doing the same things. I've always believed "If it ain't broke, don't try to fix it." That adage is the philosophy of this game."

Looking at my watch, I knew our time was up.

"Girls, let's go out there and finish them off. This is a team effort. I want to see the bench active, clapping, and cheering for your teammates. I saw a few droopy heads during the first half and this disturbs me greatly. I want to see positive attitudes regardless of whether you're in the game or not. Do you understand?"

With that bit of last-minute advice, we returned to the court and were greeted by a bunch of happy, cheering fans. Our cheerleaders even had them on their feet, chanting school favorites. The pressure had become more intense as the crowd indulged itself in this heated battle.

Our defense did the job in the third quarter, as Murphy County did not score until the 3:52 mark when they hit a free throw. Our girls outscored them 13-3 in the quarter and went on to a 53-40 victory. Every girl on the team, including those who started the game on the bench, received a fair amount of playing time. This was definitely a team effort that would go down in history as our biggest win of the season.

The celebration party in the locker room is one experience I'll never forget. The sweet taste of victory for this young group of hard-working athletes was like indulging in a gigantic piece of chocolate birthday cake loaded with icing. You savor every bite because you don't want it to end.

"Girls, I am very proud of you. This ballgame tonight has proved a lot of things to a lot of people. First, it definitely proves my strong belief that teamwork and a winning attitude can beat athletic ability. Second, it proves that each of you, as an individual player, is replaceable. When called to serve duty, substitutes can step their game up a notch and stand in the gap.

"Don't ever get the idea the team couldn't make it without you. This attitude destroys teams all the time—it's like venom to the human body—it spreads throughout and poisons the interior parts unless the proper medication is taken.

"Tonight, a few of us have had to swallow a pretty large and bitter dose of humility. Regardless of how bad it seemed while being swallowed, the end result is being healed and healthy. We're an enriched and stronger team, a team that Coach Barkley and I could not be prouder of."

Whatever this story is worth to you, it was a time of learning for us. The old saying that "if you are a good coach, your team won't have any problems" is a myth. Adversity builds character. It makes any player analyze what he or she is doing and work to contribute to the success or failure of the program.

Hard times force a team to refocus, gain composure, and meditate on what action needs to be taken to see a positive outcome. But it's not always easy or enjoyable going through these times.

I found out rather quickly that a coach has to make critical decisions everyone is not going to agree with. On the front end, putting some of our starters on the bench seemed like a foolish mistake to the spectators, who could not understand why I would make such a radical lineup change for such an important game.

But they didn't realize what we had witnessed as a team and as a coaching staff over the past several days. Neither did they understand the underlying factors involved in the decision. This is when a coach just prays that his or her decision turns out to be successful, for if it doesn't, you may be admitted to the funny farm the following day.

Players' parents have a difficult time accepting change, especially when it involves their daughter or son. And, boy, do they let you know how strongly they disagree with your actions. This is the part of coaching that I find the most uncomfortable.

Parents want their kids to be the best, and I'm sure every parent on Earth does and should feel this way. However, when it comes to sports, the coach has to make decisions for the betterment of the team, not just for Sally, Judy, Megan, John or David, and this is where the problems begin.

After this win, I was on Cloud Nine. I wasn't even sure I could sleep that night. However, I quickly learned that a parent was very upset about my decision to put her daughter on the bench. And, for several days, the mother and daughter didn't speak to me.

This was devastating to me but, at the same time, a learning experience. I finally realized I had to do what I had to do, regardless of whose toes I stepped on. I felt good about my decision and I had to be responsible for the outcome, be it good or bad. Even though we were victorious, and it was a big win at that, some were still not satisfied.

The mother, the daughter and I patched things up over time, and we went back to business as usual. But I'm not sure things were ever as good as they once were between us.

Nevertheless, throughout my first year, I was made aware of the two lifestyles of a coach. It's not all glory and stardom. It is some of what I believe to be the most difficult work I have ever been associated with.

Dealing with parents (and other family members), players, the administration, the community, and being true to your own personal values and deep-rooted beliefs for the game are stupendous tasks to juggle. But fulfilling ones, nonetheless.

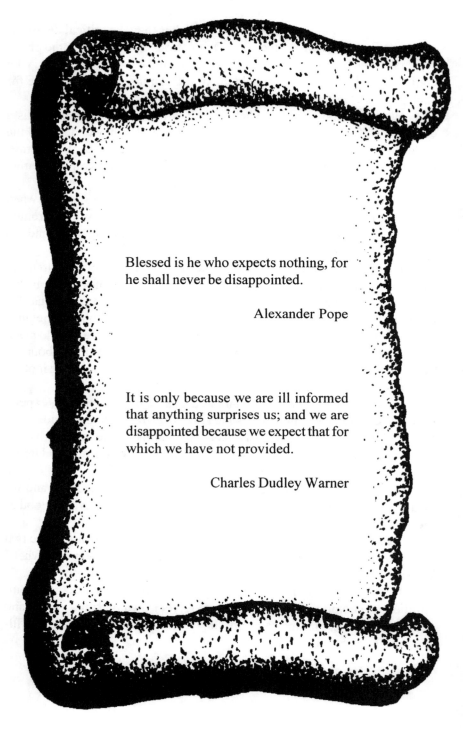

Blessed is he who expects nothing, for he shall never be disappointed.

Alexander Pope

It is only because we are ill informed that anything surprises us; and we are disappointed because we expect that for which we have not provided.

Charles Dudley Warner

Teacher Expectations

6

While attending a summer leadership conference, I was put into a small huddle-group with several people from around the Southeast. Between each large group session, we would meet in our small groups to discuss topics on a more personal, in-depth level.

As several ideas were tossed around, the discussion turned to education, and, more specifically, educators. One noble gentleman stated society expected far too much of educators. His words were my cue to put my feelings into perspective.

"I think you are exactly right, sir. We have such a high calling to be a great leader and example to the youth of today. However, not only are we to teach the academic principles to them and evaluate to see that given material has been internalized, but we are also faced with an epidemic of social problems to contend with."

Before I could finish my train of thought, I was rudely interrupted by another gentleman exclaiming, "But those problems are not yours to deal with. You must be solely concerned with teaching the student sound curriculum objectives. Those problems must stay outside the classroom. If they need help, let them work them out at home, or else go to the guidance counselor. That's their job."

I honestly could not believe my ears. Who was this man? What authority did he have on the subject? Had this guy ever really taught school? Did he have children? Was he tuned in to their lifestyle, to know the variety of stresses plaguing them every day? Was this guy in touch with reality?

I quickly offered a rebuttal.

"Most of these kids are in homes where their needs are not being met. The number of single-parent families, broken homes, and dysfunctional families is escalating and all needs are not being dealt with properly. The breakdown of the family unit has caused tremendous moral, social and economic problems.

"On the whole, children tend to have lower social standards and values now than ever, which has led to increasingly higher teenage pregnancy rates, drug abuse problems, violence and incidents of theft. This, in turn, becomes an economic problem due to the government having to fund a vast majority of these teen mothers through welfare, funding rehabilitation for drug addicts, and expansion of prisons and juvenile homes to house these kids. All of this means higher taxes for the consumer, which is an added stress for today's family.

"Furthermore, I am concerned about each student as an individual. If we do not recognize these needs, then we are ignoring the obvious and turning our backs on our future leaders. Problems must be dealt with properly. Sometimes we only have one chance to befriend a teen who is crying out for help, and that may be my student who comes to fifth period class late in tears and then proceeds to fall asleep for the remainder of class. This same student may then proceed to go home, wallowing in his or her lake of problems, and then self-destruct, maybe even to the point of suicide."

Continuing, I said, "What good is it if I lecture this student about facts and figures, forcing him or her to pay attention to this most important lesson, if I lose this student tonight to suicide or a drug overdose?"

"Don't misunderstand me, sir. I cannot solve the world's problems or even attempt to do so. But if I am in a situation where I am given the opportunity to take a moment to counsel a student through a painful time, I am compelled to do so. We are mandated to report abusive situations brought to us by students. We must go through a referral process to Human Services if we know or have physical reason to believe a student is in an abusive situation."

Again he prodded, "You let the guidance office deal with these items. It's not often that those situations arise, and you should refer them to the school counselor."

"From your final comment," I said, "It's obvious you are not a teacher! And, by the way, what is your occupation ... and your reason for attending this conference?"

As he settled in his seat he got a very matter-of-fact look on his face and said, "I have a Ph.D. in education. My entire educational process has been a conclusive study on education. And through my experiences, I have found and firmly believe educators spend too much time on things other than teaching. We need to get our minds directed back to the basics of this profession. We have gotten off-course and are continuing to see a decline in the quality of education as I once knew it."

"Quite frankly," I replied, "I can probably agree with the last part of your statement. I feel sure you have seen immense changes over the years, but what I'm not so sure about is your perception of the way these changes should be handled. You seem to be a scholar of the 'old school' and maybe even a top graduate from this ideology, but, in short, this theory does not stand true today. It just does not work.

"Seeing that our nation has seen a recent 180-degree shift in attitudes, values, morals and authority lines for teenagers, we have a lot more to contend with, on the whole, than in previous years. Even since I graduated from high school in 1988, things have greatly changed, or might I say, worsened in most areas for kids overall.

"Kids have more freedom, more free time, more money (which means newer and more cars; more money for substance abuse expenditures), but much lower expectations and motivation toward educational endeavors.

"They have a hard time staying focused, even for a 45-50 minute block of time, much less concentrating on their future goals. These kids live for today and today only. No thought about tomorrow—none whatsoever. It's all a matter of short-term thinking: What can I do to make me feel good or keep me from feeling bad now?

"The word *patience* is a foreign term for these teens. That's the root of the big problems of abuse, sexual promiscuity and crime. They don't understand solving problems takes precious time. Finishing school takes many years, sex can and should wait till marriage, and it takes an education and a good job to produce money to buy all the material goods they need and want. This whole process takes time—you don't have to experience it all now. But the pressure placed on teens to achieve these things, mainly by their peers, is alarming.

"Going back to your point about academics, I will agree that academics are on my top priority list as a teacher. I spend the greater portion of my class time dispersing the required information about the subject matter. It is my heart's desire for each student to pay close attention, take careful notes, ask intriguing questions, and see success on quizzes and tests. But first and foremost, I want my kids to come alive in my class, to actually enjoy the time we spend together, to get and stay focused, and actually learn something they can use in their future lives.

"In order to do this, the teacher has to have an openness when he or she is approached by the students to discuss problems which extend beyond the classroom. And believe me, kids truly know if you're concerned about their whole person, or if you're merely focused on your class requirements and act as if they are machines and shut yourself down to any personal interactions. I'm just an advocate of keeping your eyes and ears wide open at all times and being resourceful to the students.

"It would be absurd to expect a guidance counselor to be accessible to each student at all times. They already have job overload with all the paper work involving grades, scholarships and interaction with parents. We must pull together and each take an active part of being involved in counseling situations.

"Furthermore, teens are at a stage in their lives when they really need to feel loved. They need to be shown love—not just told. This needs to be carried into the schools because so many of these kids are not getting it at home—they are literally starving to death for attention! I feel the educator must play a vital role in seeing that some part of this emotional need is met."

"I totally disagree," he murmured. "You are young ... once you've been at this a while you'll see what I'm talking about."

"If being an educator produces these types of attitudes with years of experience, I hope I am not around in this career too much longer to be infiltrated in such a negative way. I think it's all a matter of what is individually experienced that shapes our attitudes toward the 'do's and don'ts' in education.

"And lastly, I think it would be a good idea for you to revisit a high school. Go back and reacquaint yourself with the real world of a high school full of teenagers and have your eyes reopened. I firmly believe if you are not presently in a situation, it is hard to have an accurate perception.

"You are at a different level in the collegiate realm. You do not experience the day-in, day-out lifestyle of a high school teacher. I encourage you, or might I challenge you, to visit and interact with some high schools. There might be a slight possibility you could have your heart broken over some of the sad realities our teens are facing."

Whether you agree with my viewpoint or the gentleman's, the same facts remain. No one person is always right about what it takes to be a "good teacher," nor is there ever going to be complete agreement on how much involvement should take place in the personal lives of a student. These topics have been debated for years and will continue, I am sure.

But my experience has proven that teachers are expected to play a variety of roles by various people. Mentioned below are some of the most common ones brought to my attention.

1. ***Teacher.*** First and foremost, my job is that of a teacher. A teacher is the leader who gives information that should be learned, or at least ideally this is supposed to happen. But society says not only are you to teach, you are to make sure the students learn the material, and you will be held responsible.

   The big question I've often wondered is, "How do I make or see to it that another kid learns?"

   I think that means internalizing it, or memorizing, or something like that. What a big responsibility to teach, and then to evaluate how much has been learned.

2. ***Parent.*** The term is "in loco parentis," that is, acting as a parent in lieu of a parent or when the parent is absent. We teachers are also the disciplinarians while students are at school. Students ask us the questions, everything from leaving class to use the restroom to borrowing forgotten lunch money, and then we must give the appropriate answer. We serve as temporary parents for the school day.

   When discipline codes are broken, the teacher, along with the administration and its rules, must govern what action is to be taken. Corporal punishment? Detention? Suspension? Alternative school? The tough decisions must be made based upon our better judgment, just as parents must do when their kids are at home.

3. ***Counselor-Psychologist.*** As discussed earlier in the chapter, I feel very strongly that each and every teacher must be able to counsel a student if the need arises. We are expected to take care of a building full of teenagers each and every day, and part of this care-giving should involve open communication lines be-

tween student and teacher. This can then become the channel for problems to be discussed and sorted out. However, teachers cannot and should not try to solve the world's problems. Rather, teach by example and direct students in a more positive manner.

4. ***Friend-Confidant.*** If only teachers could learn to be friends to their students. Notice that I did not say buddies, but friends; persons who genuinely care about others' wellbeing and make every effort possible to meet the needs of the others. Gaining friendship with all students is impossible; however, we should strive to achieve this because teachers are stereotyped by society as being "friendly," nice, and caring—like no other profession today.

On the other hand, we are expected to be a confidant. Kids expect us to keep everything that happens within the confines of our class period confidential. Maybe this rule should stand, or maybe it shouldn't.

Nevertheless, I have observed this first year that most teachers talk among themselves about kids' grades, sports, behavior problems and potential to be good leaders, and this always makes for interesting conversation over lunch.

On the other hand, I rarely hear a teacher exploit personal matters. A line needs to be formed at some point in the friend-confidant relationship, and I believe the responsibility of forming it falls on the shoulders of the professional.

5. ***Nurse-Doctor.*** Regardless of what happens at school, we are supposed to be able to fix it. A kid cuts his finger, we are to provide a Band-Aid. A student has a headache, we supply Tylenol or some other mild painkiller. A kid complains of a blister on his hand, we are expected to have hydrogen peroxide and a sterile needle to pop it so it will feel better.

A kid has a runny nose, pull out the Puffs (no Puffs? I can't stand to use toilet paper ... it hurts my nose). A kid has a hangnail or breaks a nail, we are to provide clippers and emery boards for a "quick fix" till they get home, and these days it's even a good idea to keep a bottle of saline solution for the kid whose contact lens has come out and who can't get it back in.

Whew! Sounds tiring, doesn't it? And then to try to teach these kids something before their class period is over—I sometimes feel like I'm operating one of those walk-in clinics where medical services are rendered at any time.

But now there is an even greater problem. With all the uproar about AIDS, we have several new guidelines to follow when a request is made for medical attention. All teachers are advised to have rubber gloves in their desks, in the event of an emergency requiring you to handle a child who is bleeding. We no longer give out medication of any kind, not even Tylenol. Too many lawsuits and problems have occurred over the years, so we have basically adopted a "hands-off" policy.

6.   *Mentor-Role Model.* Believe it or not, like it or not, as a teacher you are a role model, be it a good or a bad one. Students are watching you and paying close attention to your every move. They observe very closely, especially when things are not going so well, just to see how you'll respond under the heat of pressure. Kids basically want to like their teachers, and this puts a lot of pressure on the teacher to be simultaneously harsh enough to earn the full respect of the students and have a likable nature.

For years, teachers have been stereotyped as good, solid citizens who are upright, moral, and somewhat religious people. And that, I assume, is where the teacher "Rules of 1920" came from.

It is a bit humorous to look back at a few of the rules for educators in earlier times. I'm still not quite sure who wrote these originally, but they have been passed down to all teachers at some point or the other at a conference or in-service training. They are as follows:

1.   You will not marry during the term of your contract.

2.   You are not to keep company with men.

3.   You must be home between the hours of 8 p.m. and 6 a.m. unless attending a school function.

4.   You may not loiter downtown in ice cream stores.

5.   You may not travel beyond the city limits unless you have permission of the chairman of the board.

6. You may not ride in a carriage or automobile with any man unless he is your father or brother.

7. You may not smoke cigarettes.

8. You may not dress in bright colors.

9. You may under no circumstances dye your hair.

10. You must wear at least two petticoats.

11. Your dresses must not be any shorter than two inches above the ankle.

12. To keep the school room neat and clean, you must sweep the floor at least once daily, scrub the floor at least once a week with hot, soapy water, clean the blackboards at least once a day and start the fire at 7 a.m. so the room will be warm by 8 a.m.

And we think we have a strict code of rules to follow! I am not sure there would be anyone majoring in education if these were still the rules.

But there is a strong point to be made from these lists. Teachers are to be noble, outstanding, law-abiding citizens held in high esteem within the community in which they live or teach. Then, and only then, can teachers be a true and living example to the students we give our lives for.

Maybe I should have written a separate book on teacher expectations, since there are endless topics I could write about. But I think from these few, brief examples my point has been clearly made. Teachers are expected to play a variety of roles and are expected to fix all sorts of problems originating from some other area in a student's life.

We send our kids to school and expect the teachers to take care of everything. Teachers are expected to take care of all the things that should be taught at home, within the family or at church. All these things should be dealt with individually.

As hard as I tried to be a do-all, fix-all teacher my first year, I began to be totally consumed in the midst of it all. I did want to fix all the problems and make everything OK, but it was just not possible. I started to take these various problems home with me to toss and turn in my head, a situation that usually resulted in a sleepless night. I became so involved that all I did was think of school and how I could better myself, my classes and my kids.

Teachers are people, too! Teachers actually have, or least try to have, a normal life. They buy groceries at the store, buy clothes at the mall, shop for toiletries and other necessary products at discount stores, and are allowed to eat in ordinary restaurants. The reaction of a student when I run into him or her at the grocery store never ceases to amaze me.

"What are you doing here, Miss Ledford?" as if I were a foreign object.

"Like, I thought you were a teacher. I didn't expect to see you here!"

And my reply is always, "I'm buying groceries. I have to eat too, you know!"

Kids are always taken aback by that answer. It's really hard for them to believe we are ordinary people with ordinary lifestyles, and that we even wear ordinary clothes like cut-off shorts, T-shirts and sandals. Boy, does it really freak out a student to see you in this "strange" attire, especially if they see you without your makeup on. You are likely to be the hot topic at school the next day.

It never fails. The one time you make a mad dash to the grocery store at 11:00 p.m. to grab a gallon of milk for tomorrow's breakfast, you'll round the corner to hear, "Miss Ledford! Is that really you? You look totally different without your makeup on!"

Such experiences are part of what being a teacher is all about. And as long as I stay a part of this intriguing career, I'll be expecting all this and more.

Those who don't read have no
advantage over those who can't.

Kids Will Not Read!

7

"Open up your books and turn to page 270, chapter 16 in the *Creative Living Books* on the tables. I want you to read this chapter very thoroughly and then we'll discuss the main ideas in the reading."

"Read the chapter? Come on, Miss Ledford—we hate to read. Just let us go ahead and do the questions at the end of the chapter. This is wasting our time. Nobody's gonna read it anyway!"

"I hope I do not have to repeat the assignment. I have asked you to read the chapter and I expect you to do so. And by the way, we are not doing the questions at the end of the chapter. We will be having a quiz over the reading in thirty-five minutes. For your sake, use your time wisely."

Silence.

Either I had prompted a few kids to read who actually cared about their grades, or I had made the group mad. Nevertheless, a quiet environment was in order, until ...

"Miss Ledford?"

"Yes, Ashleigh."

"Let's read 'round robin' if we're gonna have to read. I just can't concentrate on this. I'm about to go to sleep, anyway. If we read out loud, everybody will have to keep up. I like it better that way."

" 'Round robin'? We are in a predominantly junior-senior child development class and you want to read 'round robin'?"

For a moment, I couldn't believe the request just made of me. Did I expect too much of my high school students to ask them to read a short, twelve-page chapter in which illustrations took up almost half the pages? Was I being unreasonable to require them to stay awake and focused for thirty minutes to read a section of material on the unit of study we were in? I don't know about you, but I thought this "round robin" method was too elementary for high school students!

As I tried to refocus my attention on the comment at hand, I replied, "It is not very often we do in-class reading assignments. Since we only have a classroom set of textbooks, we are forced to do all reading in class. There is some very important information which must be attained from the book, and this is just one of those days I am asking you to read a short section.

"And, no, we are not going to read 'round robin.' I have tried this before and it seems to be quite unsuccessful. It's hard for most people to comprehend when being read aloud to."

After seemingly an hour of rebuttal on this reading assignment, I allowed no further comments on the subject. The assignment had been given and now the choice was theirs—to read or not to read.

Not surprisingly, I had a few who chose the latter option. One student in particular was quite a pro at propping up his book and sitting at just the proper angle to make me think he was reading when, in fact, he was trying to sleep. All of this drama and effort was being extended just to dodge a simple reading assignment, with the end result being a zero for the day's work.

"O.K., class. Let's close our books, push them to the center of the table and get out a clean sheet of paper for the quiz."

"We're having a quiz over the reading? We don't have enough time left for the quiz! I didn't get finished reading the chapter. But if we don't do well, you're not really gonna count this grade, are you?"

"Question number one: Give me a brief description of what the chapter was about."

In the midst of the silence, I think I heard two heartbeats—the other twenty-two students had just died.

"Question number two: Tell me one thing in particular that you read."

We were down to one heartbeat.

"Question number three: Tell me one thing you learned as a result of today's assignment. Be sure to put your name on your papers and turn them in as you leave. Good-bye! See you tomorrow!"

As I hurriedly took their papers, I could see regret, disbelief, and, in some instances, a don't-care attitude on their faces. Did they take this first-year teacher lightly when I said there would be a quiz at the end of class? Did they actually think they could talk me out of it when the time came? Or were they just disappointed that Child Development was actually going to require some in-class reading assignments just like all their other courses?

I was a bit disturbed myself. Why are kids not reading in today's society? They have no focus, attention spans are very short, and the desire is no longer present to discover new and meaningful experiences. What happened to the excitement of sitting down with a good book, soaking in the details of the story, and frantically reading to the end?

As I further evaluated the situation, I concluded that our society is no longer encouraging kids to read as it once did. Our electronic society (television, movies, radios, CD's, cassette tapes and video games) and the whole influx of this great importance on music, have lead to the decline of reading among children. Kids no longer need to read because so many other great inventions, ideas, and activities have come along to occupy their minds and time.

The statistics on the world's reading population and illiteracy rates ring loudly in my ears. In the U.S. alone, 60 percent of seventeen-year-olds have inadequate reading, writing and math skills that limit their chances for employment. Seven of ten high school students have difficulty writing a letter, seeking employment or requesting information. Three of five twenty-year-olds are unable to read a map or total their lunch bill. And one of eight seventeen-year-olds has reading and writing skills below the sixth grade level (they're functionally illiterate).

Illiteracy places youth at risk for other social problems: 68 percent of arrested youth, 85 percent of unwed mothers, 75 percent of welfare dependents, 85 percent of dropouts and 72 percent of the unemployed are functionally illiterate (*Making the Grade*, 1989).

We have a tremendous problem on our hands that I'm deeply concerned about. Now more than ever, kids need to be exposed to reading. So what is an educator to do? I'll share a few ideas I've learned over this past year as a beginning teacher.

First of all, I developed a free reading program for my students. I found an old magazine rack and filled it with subscriptions I felt catered to the teen scene. These magazines were on display in the front of the room for my students to enjoy before or after class, and when all work had been completed. Even on test days, those who finished early were permitted to choose a magazine to read while their peers completed the exam.

I also used free reading time as an incentive for rewarding good over-all classroom behavior. And, believe it or not, it did work.

The rules were clear—this free reading time was a privilege. In order for it to continue, class time must be devoted to completing assignments on time and reading in-class material quietly until finished. Also, classroom behavior had to remain good. I felt this was a fair deal, and overall a positive experience for the students and myself.

Secondly, I wanted to encourage reading outside the classroom. I also wanted the students to search for information on the subjects they were studying.

To achieve these goals, I assigned research articles on various occa-sions. A research article assignment consisted of the student looking for an article from a given list of topics and then clipping it, reading it thoroughly, pasting it to a piece of notebook paper and writing a summary and reaction report.

For example, in my Child Development class, the topics included parenting issues, prenatal development, childbirth methods, or anything re-garding statistics on teenage pregnancy. The student would look through the daily newspapers, old or recent magazines or other reading materials to find a piece of information on the topic.

After clipping and pasting, the student would write a one-page report that included an overall summary of the article and concluded with his or her reaction to the article. The latter part of the report was a chance for the students to express themselves about the research and offer any emotion or wisdom they might have had on the subject.

The best part of all was, I thoroughly enjoyed reading them. This was a time when grading was fun and educational for me, as I learned new and updated information.

Overall, the kids seemed to benefit from this activity. Many of the students would rush into class on the day their research was due and ex-claim, "Miss Ledford, did you know that? I can't believe it! ... and I found out that ... I can't wait for you to read my article and paper."

What an exciting experience to see kids eager about their assign-ments. It was almost like they had discovered a lost treasure. Many of them were reading out of the newspaper or other periodicals for the very first time. We need to be active readers—all of us. And projects of this nature somehow have a way of making the process more exciting.

Third, I began to plan lessons involving the library. Scheduling a class period or two each semester that required spending some time finding or researching material in the library proved beneficial to my students.

In the beginning, the students took offense at the idea of having to do "research" for a home economics course. The thought of having to dig for material didn't excite them in the least. But we managed to survive.

Students were required to do research projects on various architectural styles in Housing and Interiors class, look up specific birth defects for Child Development, find the differences in various types of families and statistics on each in Home Economics II, the alarming statistics surrounding teenage pregnancy in my Adult Living course, and provide information on a specific career of their choice in Home Economics I.

With so many interesting topics for research, the library proved to be a valuable asset. If nothing else, I wanted to familiarize kids with another source of free reading material.

Fourth and finally, I encouraged reading by supporting our school book fair. I allowed my kids to attend the fair during class time. Going to the fair gave the students an opportunity to browse through a varied selection of reading material geared for their age level, and they loved it. Then, I allowed them time to get acquainted with their new purchases by devoting the remainder of the class period to free reading.

Mentioned above are some of the things I used in my program to help students further develop their reading skills. I realize not all kids will enjoy reading, just as all kids don't enjoy math. But it is a crucial area that has been overlooked for far too long.

Reading must be a big part of each and every curriculum in order for kids to see its usefulness. It can be fun and exciting if only presented in the proper manner.

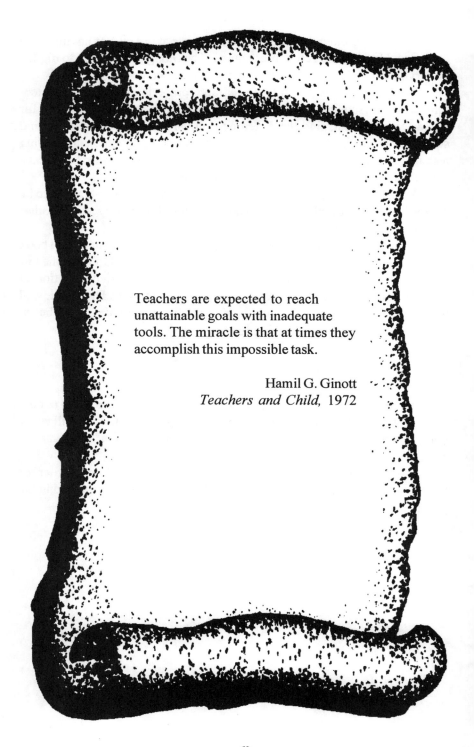

Teachers are expected to reach
unattainable goals with inadequate
tools. The miracle is that at times they
accomplish this impossible task.

Hamil G. Ginott
Teachers and Child, 1972

Where's My Teacher Handbook?

8

The morning tardy bell had just finished its shrill eight-second ring as I prepared to call the roll. It was another haywire morning, with all the problems of a typical day, until Renee burst in the door late.

"Miss Ledford, I've been talking to my English teacher and she said you were averaging my grades wrong. If you were averaging them like Mrs. Williams does hers, I would have a B+ instead of a B. She says you need to correct this immediately!"

I guess I was shocked more than I was angered by this statement, since it caught me by surprise.

"Renee, first of all, my grading procedures are done exactly as my mentor teacher and the principal's wife have shared with me. I think you must be confused on the method I am using, but I promise it will come out the same, even if the calculation is different between Mrs. Williams and me. Nevertheless, this will not be a disruption at this time. Class has begun, and I will discuss this with you at the end of the period if you would like."

As Renee sank down into her seat, I continued with class, disturbed all the while by her comment.

? ? ?

It really amazes me that we give kids a handbook and continually send home memos, letters and reminders so kids and parents will be "informed," but administrators fail to realize the needs of the new teacher, who is clueless.

A fully equipped manual, one that could instruct and guide new teachers, is badly needed. Throwing new teachers into an average high school without any written instructions is like throwing a hunk of raw meat into a den of lions—it is certain to be devoured.

I'm sure there is someone somewhere reading this chapter who was blessed enough to have been given a handbook of this nature at the onset of their career by the school in which they were employed. But the majority of teachers (including me) didn't receive this information, which is vital to understanding the daily do's and don'ts, general operations and correct procedures for emergencies at a particular school.

A handbook should be designed to guide and answer questions for the first-year teacher. Not only will it be referred to upon orientation to the system, but it should be compiled in a format suitable for use as a continual reference.

I think each and every school operates as a unique entity, so handbooks would be different for each school. But I'm sure some basic information would be very similar (for example, procedures in the event of a tornado, fire, or some other emergency).

Listed below are some questions that remained unanswered throughout my first year. To be quite honest, I'm still not sure if I handled most of these in the proper manner.

1. ***Grading Systems.*** At my school it seemed as though everyone had a different method of calculating their students' grades. Even though we were given a percentage breakdown, the methods by which teachers arrived at scores varied considerably. Moans and groans from students as they went from class to class getting their grades constituted a common disruption we had to contend with.

    I believe there should be one formula to arrive at grades for all classes. This would eliminate all the confusion over different grading procedures.

2. ***Fire-Tornado Drills.*** If a real emergency of this kind ever happened, most schools would be in pure chaos. Which door do you exit? Do you open or close the window, and who is assigned to do that? Do you have your roll book accessible so you can re-

trieve it to get a class count when you're outside the building? Do you know which wall to line your students against and the proper position for them to be in to protect their heads?

All these questions and more weigh on a first-year teacher. Strict rules and regulations need to be given at the beginning of the year.

3. ***Bomb Threats.*** This seems to be a new fad for high school kids. We missed three half days of school due to this sporting event. The principal would broadcast over the intercom and say, "At this time, all teachers and students must exit the building."

This produced a big scare the first time it happened and kids began to gather their personal belongings, but on the second and third occasions they quickly realized this was just another false alarm and they took it as a joke. Kids would linger in the halls, leave their purses on the table and say, "I wonder how long it will take this time?"

In my opinion bomb threats need to be taken very seriously. Kids should act as though it were a tornado or fire drill, with preset guidelines (as listed in the handbook) and proper procedures implemented.

4. ***Dismissing Students.*** Since we had bells only in the morning and afternoon, there were constant problems revolving around dismissing kids at the end of the period.

Our school was equipped with clocks in each room that were supposedly set for the same time, but they would malfunction and be out of sync more times than not. Because of this, we had to rely on our own watches to monitor the time as closely as possible.

Obviously if you have thirty-five faculty members you have thirty-five watches, each set just a bit differently, a situation that led to students being let out of class at different times. If only we had had a class period bell system ... what a difference that would have made.

5. ***Absentees and Tardies.*** There has to be a cut-and-dried rule, for this problem has cropped up at every school in the country.

When is a kid absent from your class? Well, there's no doubt if they miss your class they're absent, but it becomes much more confusing than this.

If a kid is dismissed twenty minutes into a fifty-minute class period, is he counted as absent because he did not stay for half of the class? Is he counted as tardy for leaving early, or do you just let it slide because he was there almost half the time and, after all, what is four or five more minutes?

Nationwide this controversy has been a hot topic among educators. This sort of problem could be resolved if everyone adhered to the same rules that should be outlined (again, in the teachers handbook) and strictly enforced by the administration.

It is so unfair for one teacher to mark a student tardy for walking in the door as the bell rings, while another teacher allows a student to be dismissed with thirty minutes remaining in the class with no adverse consequences.

6. ***Hall Passes and Interruptions.*** This is probably the most annoying problem teachers must contend with on a daily basis. Do you allow kids to go to the restroom during class? Do you have an "emergency only" policy and, if so, how do you monitor this "emergency only"?

Do you provide tissues in your room or do you allow a kid to be temporarily dismissed to blow his or her nose in the restroom? Do you keep a running chart of your female students' "personal problem" requests to go to the restroom, so the privilege is not abused every week or two instead of every month?

You must have clear-cut answers for these requests, and you have to be careful about who you grant and deny these requests to, for if you give one person permission, someone else will surely say, "You let 'so and so' go, so why can't I go?"

Hall passes have been and always will be a headache. And speaking of headache, interruptions from other students (and teachers) can and will be a problem if you don't nip them in the bud. Requests to sew up football uniforms, wash gym clothes and sick room sheets, store lunches in refrigerators, provide safety pins and lend out measuring tapes were a continual menace.

I could not believe what was being asked of me on a daily basis—as if I did not have anything better to be doing. I'm not sure if first-year teachers have more interruptions or not, but it seemed to me that I was getting hit harder than some of my colleagues.

7. ***Sending a Kid to the Office, Sick Room, or out Into the Hall.***
I am convinced there are certain times a student should always be sent to the office, the sick room or removed from class. I know all the classroom management techniques say a teacher should handle almost any situation by himself or herself without office referral, if possible. This is an excellent theory, but we must take a closer look at it.

I'm an advocate of teacher control in the classroom. I rarely sent a student to the office and, if I did, it was in a situation I believed needed to be handled by the principal or vice-principal. But I think there should be some hard and fast rules (stated in the handbook) for such situations.

Here are a few suggestions I propose:

■ **Office Referrals**

If a student is in any way harming another student's body—be it in a fight, trying to burn another with a lighter or matches, or a premeditated action to invoke harm—it should immediately be an office referral.

A student who possesses tobacco of any kind, drugs, alcohol or weapons should be sent to the office immediately. Too many teachers see these things and say "put that up," treating the situation so lightly that students mock them and joke about the teachers' remarks.

■ **Sick Room**

A student who is bleeding or who shows outward signs of being sick, vomiting or feverish should be sent.

■ **Removal from Class**

If students are distractions to those around them or to any part of the class, send them. We as educators cannot allow class clowns to disrupt the majority. It is our responsibility to remove the kids for the betterment of the class.

These suggestions could be very useful and help produce a less-than-chaotic academic environment. At the beginning of each school term, with input from interested teachers, a handbook could be produced for all teachers to follow.

? ? ?

As I think through the many times I was unsure of what to do, I see a clear need for a handbook of this nature. I cannot imagine the stress that could have been reduced from my daily schedule if I had only had an outline to follow. And, by the way, why was I never told so many of these little nit-picky things about the field I had studied for four years?

Survival List
for New Teachers
(what I wish someone had
told me years ago)

FAST FOOD HAT:
moonlighting to
make ends meet

SMILE:
her good
humor gets
her through
the day

WRINKLES:
she's 35, but
aging after 10
years in the
classroom.

**'Dynamics of
Testing':**
a little light
reading for
courses she's
taking to keep
up her
certificate

TARGET:
for spitballs &
other unidentified
flying objects

**STOP
WATCH:**
so she can
keep on
schedule

SUPPLIES:
provided
through own
funds

**LETTERS TO
PARENTS:**
maybe some
of them will
show up at
parents night

COMBAT ZONE:
broke up a fight

**SCIENCE
PROJECT:**
need to feed

TRACK SHOES:
necessary for
hall and bus duty

**55 HOUR
WORK WEEK:**
stacks of papers to grade

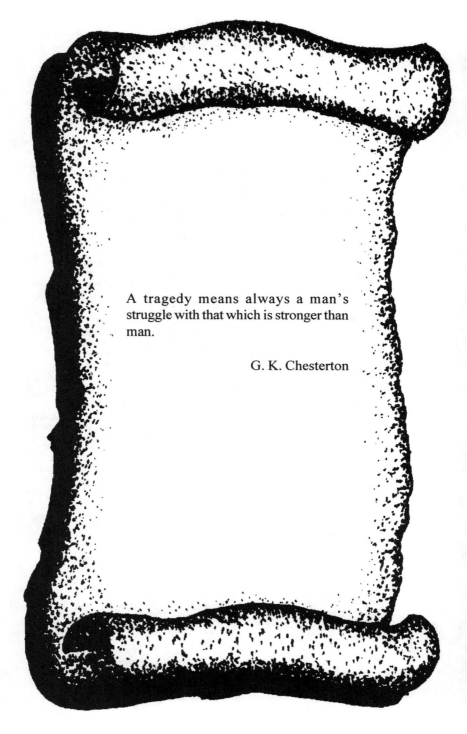

A tragedy means always a man's struggle with that which is stronger than man.

G. K. Chesterton

The Tragedies Teachers Face

9

"Hello," I mumbled, as I briefly woke up to answer the phone.

"Miss Ledford, this is Susan. I just wanted to call you and let you know that Tiffany just died. I knew she'd want you to know, so I thought I should call."

"Susan, I can't believe this. Are you OK? Where are you? What happened so quickly to change her condition? I was just at the hospital yesterday and things were about the same," I replied.

Silence. I could hear the tears muffled through the phone. I was in a state of shock, totally helpless, almost frozen in thought. Could this be a nightmare? Surely this was not really happening. All this and more went through my mind as I said good-bye and quietly hung up the phone.

Susan had just made one of the most difficult phone calls a friend could ever make. The call that comes with the news of a lost best friend.

Breaking the news to this teacher who had become very close to Tiffany over the past eight months must have been an awesome task. Hearing that a student had died due to injuries sustained in a tragic alcohol-related car accident gripped and ripped at my heart like nothing I had ever felt before.

This whole tragedy happened on the rainy evening of March 21, 1993, while I was out of the country on a short-term mission trip over spring break. When I arrived back at school on the Monday following the trip, I was greeted at the door with students explaining the details of the accident.

I was taken by surprise, as this was the first I had heard of the wreck. As I entered the office, several faculty members rushed to tell me about Tiffany and to express their hopes she was going to be OK, with time.

I hurriedly signed in and went to find Tiffany's clique of girlfriends to get more details. Ashleigh and Mary Beth were quick to explain the whole ordeal and asked if I was going to the hospital.

"She's in ICU at Erlanger, Miss Ledford. We're really worried about her. She's in the trauma unit with some really bad injuries."

As both girls talked tears formed in their eyes. They were terrified. Seeing them so concerned told me that Tiffany must be in a life-or-death situation.

I hugged them both and called the hospital to check on Tiffany's condition. I was able to reach a family member in the waiting room who seemed hopeful that Tiffany would make it through, with a lot of prayers and time to heal. They thanked me for my concern as a teacher and friend to Tiffany. I assured them I would be over right after school and softly said good-bye.

The day passed very slowly. My kids were solemn and in deep thought for most of the day. Disbelief, worry and confusion filled the faces of most of my teenage students. I wanted to comfort them, to reach out to them and assure them that Tiffany would be OK, so we talked the majority of the class period. We shared questions and concerns and prayed that time would heal everything.

Upon arriving at the hospital, I quickly found Tiffany's mom and dad. It warmed my heart for them to recognize who I was. Her mother thanked me for coming and shared with me some information that brought tears to my eyes.

"Tiffany really loved you, Miss Ledford. She came home many days telling various stories and experiences you had shared in class. She really looked up to you. In spite of all the difficulties she was going through, she knew you genuinely cared for her.

"I think you were a coach and a friend to Tiffany. She talked about you like any of her other girlfriends. I sometimes wondered how a teacher could be so involved with a student's overall life, but I felt like I already knew you.

Thanks so much for caring. It would mean a lot to Tiffany to know you are here."

Hearing all of this made me break out in a cold chill. Did I realize what a complex job I had taken on by being a teacher? Did anyone ever prepare me for an event like this? Was this emotional side of teaching ever discussed in EDCI 201, 330 or 433 in college? Did more experienced teachers, who had previously gone through such tragedies themselves, offer a word on how to deal with a situation of this nature?

The answer is no, no, no! No one warned me that educators did not have "heart insurance" coverage. Becoming so emotionally involved with everyday life situations required opening up my heart to these kids, and I did that on a day-to-day basis. There was no quick remedy, no going to the doctor and getting a prescription to soothe a torn heart. Only time and new experiences can heal these wounds, and I was learning how to cope with this "heart condition" right alongside my students.

As several other students and various friends poured in and out, I excused myself from Tiffany's parents to visit and encourage some of them. It was difficult to know exactly the right words to say, but I offered a lot of hugs and shared in several prayers with Tiffany's peers. We were all waiting to hear, hopefully, word of improvement in her condition.

The family went in to visit and reported very little change. She was in a semi-coma. Amazingly, only days after the accident and talking and responding to her family and a few friends, she had sunk into a non-responsive state, one that was hard for those who loved her so much to face—one of not knowing what was going on with Tiffany.

A couple of days passed, with reports being positive one day and negative the next. The kids at school made a computerized banner with "Get Well" sentiments on it and everyone colored it in and wrote messages and notes to Tiffany. My principal called me up to the office and asked if I would deliver the banner to Tiffany that evening. I was going to the hospital later, so he asked if I would present this to her parents.

That visit to the hospital was my last. Tiffany's parents were very appreciative of the act of kindness from her peers and smiled as they read the notes covering the banner.

"She'll really love this. This will be hanging in her room ... you just wait and see."

Tiffany lived for her friends. They were the essence of her being. They really loved her, and she loved them. I knew this, and boy, did I ever realize how much she was loved only hours after I left.

I spent most of the next day giving hugs and bits of encouragement to a load of high school kids with shattered hearts. This small country school had just lost one of its bright, popular, life-of-the-party students who could never be replaced or forgotten, and I had to help pick up the pieces.

Tiffany was not just an ordinary student. She was a dear friend to me. This was a kid I'd spent a great deal of time with and who held a very special place in my heart. She had played on the basketball team for a brief period of time, but quickly gave it up to pursue other interests. She was in my sixth period Adult Living Class, the class that consisted of her close group of girlfriends that kept me on my toes.

She was a unique individual, one I had been drawn to earlier in the year. We had talked on several occasions about the struggles teens face and how to properly cope with them. And this was the student who was at my apartment only four months before her death for a basketball Christmas party.

Oh, the Christmas party. What a blast we had with Tiffany and, of course, the rest of the team.

It was amazing to see how quickly the other girls accepted her into their circle of friends. A night of food, fun and games all contributed to the happy memories.

Tiffany won the basketball shoot-out at the party and the grand door prize, and again received all the attention from her peers. But the most heart-warming thing was the fact that we videotaped the whole evening.

We had just started the party when I remembered we still had my mom and dad's camcorder (we had borrowed it the week before). Kevin shot video for the rest of the party and, you guessed it, Tiffany was the star of the night. You might call it coincidence, but I feel an angel was present with us that evening, and the angel wanted to make sure Tiffany would not be forgotten.

Probably one of the saddest events I have ever participated in was the funeral service for Tiffany. I guess it was just something I had never thought about, or at least, I thought it would never happen to someone so close to me. I, along with my principal and another faculty member, arrived at a small, country church on top of the mountain to see several hundred students, parents, and members of the community in attendance.

That was a sight and feeling I will never forget, nor will I forget the look on Tiffany's mother's face when I gave her a copy of the Christmas party we had videotaped. As tears flowed down her face, she said, "This is all we have to see our real, live Tiffany again. Thanks so much."

I will never understand why Tiffany had to leave us, nor will I fully understand what her parents went through or how they must feel now. I'll never feel the loss quite as deeply as her friends, the ones who had known Tiffany from childhood and went to school with her.

But I will always remember how I felt—broken, at a loss for words, and emotionally distraught that I would view an empty seat in sixth period for the rest of the year. But as I saw the seat previously occupied by Tiffany, I noticed it was not empty at all, for in her place now sat an angel.

Teachers face tragedies every day. Not only did I experience the death of a student, I was bombarded with many other tragedies that were just as devastating. Somehow, I think educators are closer to such tragedies than people in other professions.

1. **Teenage Pregnancy.** Everyday in the U.S., 2,795 teens get pregnant (*A Vision For America's Future*, 1989). This is a tragedy in and of itself. There is nothing that sends chills up my spine like hearing one of my teenage girls say, "Miss Ledford, I'm pregnant!" These two simple words mean a changed lifestyle forever. It means adolescence must be put on hold to in order to become a nurturing adult, which must carry the baby for a long, nine months.

2. **Suicide.** "Miss Ledford, I just can't go on. Everything in my life is going wrong. I think I'd be better off if I just killed myself."

   Hearing a kid relate this story brings on a feeling of helplessness, but reminds me of the urgent need to help turn this kid around. The alarming statistics on teenage problems never cease to amaze me.

   For example, teenage suicide is the third leading cause of death among youth in the 15- to 24-year-old age bracket (*Vital Statistics of the U.S.,* 1990). You may wonder why. The answer is, for reasons right before our very eyes that are ignored or improperly dealt with. Our teenagers are taking their own lives at a tremendous rate.

Teachers should be concerned enough to take time away from the "open your books and do ..." method of teaching and try to help them.

3.   *Abuse and Neglect.* When I think of abuse, I'm reminded of a story that was told to me by a teacher friend of mine.

Mrs. Jones had a nice young girl in her English class who usually sat in the back of the room. As the year went by, Mary, we will call her, began to come into class and sleep.

The teacher would say to her in passing, "Mary, you need to stay awake and pay attention," but to no avail. The other students began to shy away from her and would even make comments like, "Wake up, you sleepyhead. Can't you stay awake?"

Mrs. Jones put a stop to that immediately and called Mary out into the hall. As Mary burst into tears, she explained that she was just having some problems and everything would be OK. She promised that it wouldn't happen again.

The teacher explained that she would like to help her. As Mary continued to sob, she fell into Mrs. Jones' arms and exclaimed, "I just can't stay awake, no matter how hard I try. Every night I have to get up around 2:00 a.m. and climb out my window and stay on the streets till it's time to catch the bus for school.

"My stepfather is an alcoholic and he repeatedly comes home in a drunken rage and forces me to have sex with him. I've tried to get away, but he slaps and beats me and then the experience is only more gruesome. I just couldn't stand it any longer, so I have to leave so he can't find me. He eventually passes out and sleeps it off by early the next morning."

I don't know about you, but I was dumbfounded when I heard this story. I never really realized what a student might be going through at home. I'm a bit more sensitive now to such situations.

4.   *Drug Addiction and Alcohol.* I dealt with problems involving drugs and alcohol on a fairly regular basis. Kids do not really believe that anything bad will ever happen to them.

Regardless of how much I would encourage the students to live a life free of alcohol and drugs, that was not enough. Even to share the knowledge that 3,794,000 twelve- to seventeen-year-olds admit to have used an illicit drug (Substance Abuse and Mental Health Services, 1993) or to confirm that drinking is the number one cause of death for teens according to the National Highway Traffic Safety Administration, still did not change behaviors.

I realized that all I could do was to bear witness that it is possible to live a full, exciting young life without those harmful substances.

5. ***Dropout Rate.*** One of my biggest jobs as an educator is to help provide a better future for each kid—which means helping him get that high school diploma. The dropout rate is alarming.

In our country, 25 percent of children do not complete high school (*Technology,* 1988). It breaks my heart to see a kid approach my desk with the necessary withdrawal forms from high school. I just wish I could get them to realize what a mistake they are making.

Some of the problems we are seeing are that school dropouts are more prone to be participants in crime and substance abuse, and they are more likely to become pregnant or unemployed during their working years.

6. ***Crime.*** Now more than ever kids are involved in crime. Teachers have a much greater burden when entering a school system today, as 135,000 kids each day bring guns to American schools (*The State of America's Children,* 1995). Safety is a great concern in our schools, and we are still searching for ways to reduce this massive problem.

7. ***Divorce and Stepfamilies.*** This breakdown of the family causes students to be thrown into stepfamily situations that are sometimes disturbing, unhealthy and unwanted. I deal with such problems quite often.

Students find it hard to adjust to new living arrangements with strangers invading their personal space. They are also dealing with issues including splitting time between their birth parents and the delegation of authority.

Being aware of all these problems is not enough. Teachers must be equipped with the knowledge to properly handle and effectively deal with kids who have these problems. We must face these tragedies head on and do the best possible job to help kids cope in these dire circumstances.

Our kids bring a heavy load to school with them every day. We must somehow manage to put all of it in perspective, try to teach them what we are required to teach them and hope that they learn.

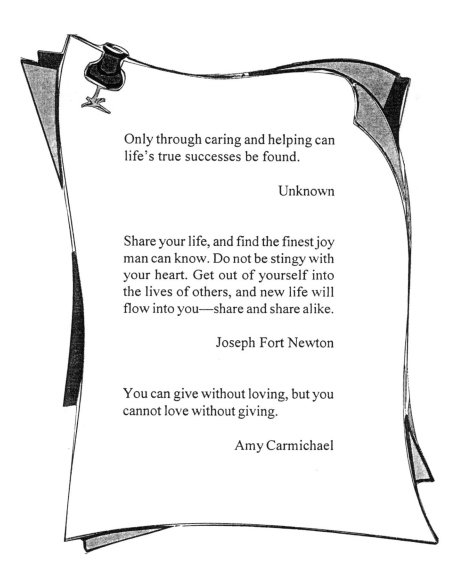

Only through caring and helping can life's true successes be found.

Unknown

Share your life, and find the finest joy man can know. Do not be stingy with your heart. Get out of yourself into the lives of others, and new life will flow into you—share and share alike.

Joseph Fort Newton

You can give without loving, but you cannot love without giving.

Amy Carmichael

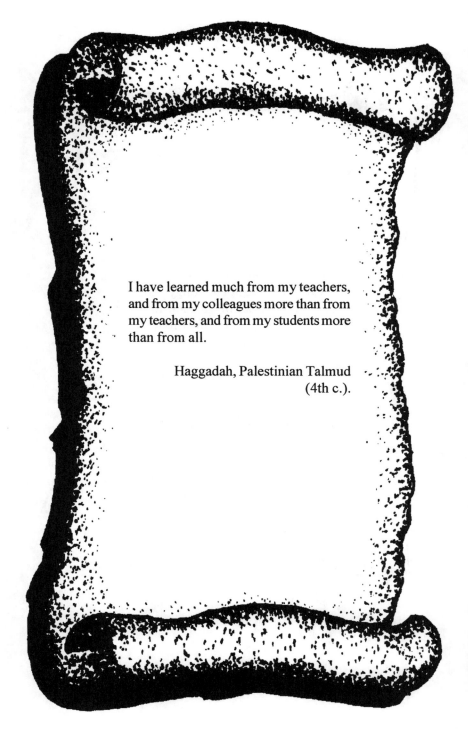

I have learned much from my teachers, and from my colleagues more than from my teachers, and from my students more than from all.

Haggadah, Palestinian Talmud (4th c.).

Getting on Eye Level with the Kids

10

As a first-year teacher, I was drawn to a few students more quickly than to others. I tended to study my classes and started unintentionally stereotyping certain individuals.

To help me with this problem, I decided to construct a simple project. I would allow my students to create small booklets about themselves.

I announced the assignment to the class and provided them with the proper materials, magazines, construction paper, glue and markers. The rest was up to the students.

Each person was assigned to create a mini-booklet about his or her life. The booklet was to be a minimum of five chapters long, with each chapter representing a different period in the student's life.

They were to use pictures, writings and illustrations to tell me who they were. They could include childhood experiences, feelings, hobbies, awards, favorite sports and achievements.

As my Adult Living class worked on their project, I grew anxious to read their books. It is always a joy for me to read about the lives of teenagers and to get to know them. I wanted to read about their goals, their aspirations and their desires.

I was particularly interested in the work of Kendra Tolliver, the only black female at this small rural high school. She was one of only two black students I had in my six classes and was rather quiet, seemingly shy in her interaction with her peers.

I wondered, "What would it feel like to be the only black female in the high school? Is life different for this minority student?" The questions continued to keep me offtrack.

As finished booklets began to be turned in, a few students asked if they could to take theirs home to complete. Some even wanted to include photos of particular events, so I agreed to extend the assignment.

The rest of the day flew by. My main focus was to get home, read Kendra's paper, and learn more about this intriguing student.

Her book was not among those I had. She must have chosen to finish at home. It would be another night before my mind would settle down.

During hall duty the next morning, Kendra brought the book to me. My eagerness made me flip it open, and Kendra began to tell her story:

> ***Chapter 1,*** age 5: (Kendra had used pictures of kids in a classroom, a ball and glove, and Michael Jordan)
>
> "I really loved school. I didn't want to go home in the evenings. I would cry each day when my mother came to pick me up. I started playing sports as a small child and I would still play sports if I thought I was good enough."
>
> ***Chapter 2,*** ages 6-11: (pictures: someone tripping over their large feet, a woman standing on a scale with one foot raised to make her lighter)
>
> "I had large feet for a girl. My classmates would have a foot-measuring contest and I would usually come in second. I was too tall, and thought I was fat, even though I wasn't. Now I'm 5'6", size 11 and weigh 142 pounds. Even now and then I sometimes have a low self-esteem."
>
> ***Chapter 3,*** age 16: (picture of Florence Griffith Joyner)
>
> "My hero is 'Flo Jo.' I'm going to give her a run for her money one day. One problem with Whiteville High School is they don't have a track team. I could run forever. The college I go to must have a track team. Of course this is just a dream, I know I shouldn't be so negative, but thinking that way makes me strive to prove myself wrong."

Chapter 4, college: (illustration of student in cap and gown)

"After high school, I plan to go to a 2-year college and then to the University of Tennessee at Chattanooga and be a physical therapist. I like being with people, big crowds of people. Each morning I do not have enough time to talk to everyone. I may come back to this area because everyone here seems accident prone."

Chapter 5, (pictures: $498 wedding dress, kids playing, a red Ferrari)

"Marriage does not have to be a factor in my life after college. It would be nice to have a small wedding. Two boys would be nice. All my friends were guys growing up—I'm partial to boys. And I'll take you for a ride in my car one day."

After reading Kendra's story, I knew that I had a job to do. I was motivated to get to know her, talk with her, and encourage her to pursue the things she was interested in, but I didn't have the courage to try.

I began to sift through her booklet and translate certain statements into what I thought she was really trying to say. My main goal was to take her aside and spend some time finding out who she really was.

The day I handed the booklets back to the students, I wrote Kendra a note on her paper asking if we could talk. She stayed after class and we began what eventually developed into a close friendship.

First of all, I found out that Kendra had very low self-esteem. She had absolutely zero confidence in herself or her abilities. She was a bit shy because of this and did not talk very much. It was like pulling teeth getting her to open up and talk with me, but the words finally came.

I encouraged her toward sports. Since she had used a picture of Michael Jordan as an illustration in her first chapter, I asked her if she liked basketball.

"Yeah, but I'm not any good."

"Kendra, I didn't ask you if you were good or not, I asked you if you liked the game."

"Yes, I love it."

Just from looking at Kendra it was obvious that she was athletic by nature. Strong, tight, bulging calves, muscular thighs, and a medium build were all necessary components for being physically fit—and to think she viewed herself as fat!

"Why don't you come out for the girls basketball team this year, Kendra? I'm going to be the assistant coach and I'd like to see what you can do."

As she looked down at the ground, she began to shake her head and said, "Miss Ledford, I don't know. I'm not very coordinated for all the things basketball requires, like dribbling, shooting ... I just don't think I could do it."

"Well, you'll never know if you don't try. Think about it and let me know—I sure would like to see you give it a shot."

It was almost time for the bell and Kendra had to get to her seventh period class.

"We'll finish this later. Go home tonight and think about what I said." Kendra raised her head, smiled, turned and walked away.

I was excited. I hoped that maybe some part of what I shared had sunk into Kendra's heart and made a difference. Even if it didn't, I planned to continue these meetings until it did.

And we did have more times when we met and talked, sometimes after school or early in the morning, before and after class ... we managed to spend time together. I began to understand Kendra and also to see her grow, grow in a way that I had not seen before.

Kendra did come out for basketball, at least for awhile. She mastered the running, but the technical drills were just not her thing.

She quickly realized that basketball was not what she wanted to do. I went along with her decision, but encouraged her to get involved in another sport.

Kendra dabbled in volleyball for a season, but finally found the sport she wanted to become involved in: softball. After a year of substitute play, she earned a starting position in right field.

Not only was she an excellent defensive player, but she became a doggone good hitter. It was exciting to watch her play. Seeing her gain confidence in her abilities and believing in herself was tremendous. It astonished me to see the determined look in her eyes and the smile on her face as she experienced a sense of accomplishment and self-worth.

Over these few short months, Kendra blossomed into a good leader for her peers. Now she was excelling in sports and academics. She was a solid B+ student, and made straight A's in my course. She was a conscientious student, always turning in projects last so she would have the extra time to do it right.

Seeing this new Kendra gave me hope that kids can really change if they're just given some attention and room to succeed. Kendra had proven that being the only black female in the high school was not going to be a deterrent to her success or possibilities for leadership. I don't know about you, but if I were the only white person in a school of black kids I would feel a bit out of place. Kendra did not.

She was born and raised in the community and members of her extended family went to school with her. Even though she had a sister and a brother, it was as though she was an only child due to the vast age difference among them.

Kendra really did not think too much about her situation—this was her hometown, the only place she had ever known. Nevertheless, she continued to impress me with how well she handled herself.

Since I taught vocational home economics courses, I was also the Future Homemakers of America sponsor. The club had not been very active at Whiteville High for several years, so I wanted to revamp the entire program.

As I solicited students to join FHA, I explained that selection of officers would be vital for the success or failure of the club. "I need students to run for office who will be strong leaders, people your peers will look up to and trust and allow to make decisions governing the club."

With that piece of advice, students started bringing in their membership dues and taking officer application forms to fill out. Surprisingly, Kendra came in sixth period, paid her dues, and then helped herself to an application.

Talking about a drastic change. Kendra was taking charge and running for office. Now I was really anticipating the election results.

As you might guess, Kendra won the presidency by a landslide. There were five candidates and the vote wasn't even close. This said a lot for Kendra and her peers. They had full confidence she should be the leader and they trusted her.

Kendra, along with the forty members of the organization, led our program to a tremendously successful year. We were one of the top clubs at the school and took part in various community, school and service projects.

At the close of the year Kendra was named "Outstanding FHA Member of the Year," along with one of her classmates. Both were deserving of the honor.

Looking back on this special relationship with Kendra, I am truly amazed at how a student can blossom when dealt with on his or her level. This situation alone should speak to educators all over our world to try and get on eye level with the students so we can understand each other much better.

One of the most rewarding parts of being an educator is the closeness that forms among certain students.

I like to be involved in the kids' lives. I long to be more than a dull, boring instructor of what is often perceived to be a "crip" home economics course. A friendship that has lasting value is a good way to make a difference in a student's life.

Many educators suggest that this idealistic imagery is impossible to achieve. They suggest that a hierarchy must be present in the teacher-student relationship.

I strongly disagree.

A common ground of authority and kinship can be found if the relationship is handled in the proper manner. Kids not only need positive role models, they need to be involved one-on-one with these leaders to successfully fashion themselves after them.

The need is great for teachers to take a high dive off of the pedestal of educational authority into the pool of unmotivated, pressured, frustrated, starving-for-attention teenagers in our school systems. Shouldn't we put the well-being of each child above the documented, standardized, data that we are seeking to pull from them? The pressure is so great to produce high test scores on the local, state, and national level that sometimes I feel the children are neglected.

It has been said that, "One good teacher in a lifetime may sometimes change a delinquent into a solid citizen" (Wylie, 1942). I firmly believe that statement.

Any action taken or word spoken can make or break a student. Kids are watching closely to see the actions and attitudes displayed by their teachers.

You are a role model whether you like it or not. Teachers are important people, with an opportunity to shape the lives of others.

It's an overwhelming responsibility.

Life is one long process of getting tired.

Samuel Butler

Thank God It's Friday!

11

It was finally sixth period, and it was Friday. Precisely one hour and thirty-two minutes until it would officially be the weekend. It was a crisp December day, the holiday spirit was encircling the students like an overgrown wreath, and anxiety could be felt as you walked into a classroom of teenagers eager to take a break from the day-in, day-out routine of school.

Against my better judgment, I had chosen to allow my Adult Living students to go into the kitchen labs and make a Christmas recipe. Since I was teaching five other lab classes at the same time, I was hesitant to put a sixth group of kids in the kitchen.

Nevertheless, it was Christmas. Christmas is a time to be generous, full of love and kindness, and trustworthy all the while.

I finally decided to make "Krispy Christmas Treats" as a way for the students to gain some experience in the lab. My innermost desire was to see the kids have a good time together, listen to Christmas carols, and have some time away from their regular class schedule.

I thoroughly explained the rules for the kitchen: Wash your hands immediately upon entering the lab. Each student must wear an apron. Absolutely no horseplay. Follow directions carefully by reading the recipe. Use only the amount of ingredients necessary, for we have exactly enough for each class to finish the day. Do not turn on the ovens—we will not be using them. Stay in your lab group. Do not wander from kitchen to kitchen, and so on.

I made every effort to ensure that each student fully understood what I expected of him. To put twenty-seven juniors and seniors in one kitchen area at one time was dangerous enough without having an accident occur due to negligence.

Time is such an important element when teaching foods. Each second must be accounted for in order to complete the lab of the day. Strict discipline is also a must. Students must cooperate with each other and do their part or the lab grade will suffer.

I rushed into the kitchen and began to help each group get started by distributing supplies.

Since there are only three basic ingredients in this recipe, margarine, miniature marshmallows and Rice Krispies, I figured this was going to be a breeze to pull off. We were molding Christmas shapes such as bells, snowmen and Christmas trees, and then decorating them with red hots and green candy sprinkles for the kids to eat and enjoy.

I needed to get the margarine and marshmallows to the kids first. As I emptied my next-to-last bag of marshmallows for the final group, I reached for the remaining bag to get it measured for my seventh period Home Economics I class. It was not there.

I searched frantically for the marshmallows and they were not to be found. I went through each lab group to see if they had been misplaced. Oh, no, I thought, the last group of freshman I promised would have lab today would not be able to cook.

I panicked. They were here just a minute ago. I knew they were. I counted out the supplies very carefully and the marshmallows were missing. The only thing left to do was question my sixth period students on the whereabouts of the missing marshmallows.

"Has anyone seen the bag of extra marshmallows sitting on top of this cabinet? They were here just minutes ago, and I must have them for my seventh period students or they will not get to have lab today. I'm serious, students. The bag must be replaced on the cabinet or I will set each of you down and labs will not be completed."

There was no movement from the kids. I was disturbed that this group of students I longed to give privileges to could let me down so easily.

Laughter came from the group in the corner. I walked over and questioned them.

"Is there something this group would like to share with me? I do not think this is funny in the least!"

As eyes began to roll and nervousness spread from student to student, I could feel the perpetrator within the group. Someone had taken the marshmallows, or at least knew something about them.

I quickly glanced at the students in the other groups and, just as I turned my head, Wham! I heard a drawer slam shut. When I reacted to the noise, Chip jumped in front of the slammed cabinet drawer with a big possum grin on his face.

"Is there something in the drawer that you would like to show me, Chip?" I asked as I headed toward him and the mystery drawer.

"No, I don't know anything about it. I swear. I didn't do it."

I opened the drawer and a gasp came from the group as I viewed the ripped bag of marshmallows.

"Stop! Everyone take a seat immediately. I mean drop what you are doing and go to your tables. We have some talking to do and you have some explaining to do!"

As I scurried through the kitchen turning off the stovetop eyes, I was furious. Here I had spent several hours grocery shopping, loading and unloading supplies and reworking lesson plans just to fit this in, not to mention the money expended from our account to finance this project.

As students continued to be seated, muffled whispers were exchanged by several of them. Guilt was written all over their faces, regardless of their cries that they were not involved. Anger was expressed by others who, in fact, were not guilty, and who, because of the actions of their peers, were unable to finish the project.

"First and foremost," I began, "I am totally disappointed in this class. You all have begged to be involved in the Christmas projects and I thought, 'My, if anybody should be mature enough to handle this, it will be my older kids.' So I bought into this idea, and what do I get in return? A thief, as I like to call it, or a prank as I'm sure you like to term this event."

"Whatever the case, dishonesty is the prime reason I have reacted in this way. I do not believe in taking another's property at any time for any reason, without prior permission—even in the food labs. What you have perceived to be a joke has now caused us to be short of supplies for the next class. Pure selfishness and non-respectful attitudes for your fellow students will not, I repeat, will not be tolerated in this class! And if I had to guess, most of you know exactly what happened, how it occurred, when it occurred and by whom. We are going to sit here until I get to the bottom of this. Now remember, this is not about a bag of eighty-nine cent marshmallows; this is about right and wrong, do's and don'ts, values and morals, honesty and dishonesty.

"Someone had to take the marshmallows off the cabinet, tear the package open, eat some of them, and then sling them into the drawer. So actually, more than one person could have been involved. Would anyone like to volunteer some information on what really happened?"

The students' eyes began to wander back and forth across the room, with shoulders shrugging as if to say they did not have a clue.

"You're only making this more difficult on yourselves. Someone, and I promise you, some person will come and tell me who committed this dishonest act. Your 'friends' are not as loyal as you may think. It may be immediately after class or it might be after school, but I'll find out. Then I'm referring you to the office for stealing. If you confess before the end of the class period, I will handle the discipline myself. Otherwise, the administration will take care of it."

Knowing my prime suspects in the group had been in previous trouble throughout the year, I thought this might scare them into coming forth and admitting they had made a mistake. As several innocent students became annoyed at the whole ordeal, they began to comment, "This is stupid. This is causing so many problems. We know who did it ... just admit it and get this thing over with."

Crystal then raised her hand and said, "I didn't do it, but I know who did."

Ooh's and ahh's from her classmates turned into deadly stares.

Dana chimed in, "Well, I didn't take or eat any of the marshmallows, but I did throw them to somebody. Now, I'm not gonna tell on him ... oops, I mean this person, but I was involved."

As Chip sank down into his seat and cut Dana a nasty look, he half-heartedly declared, "I'm the one who took the marshmallows. I'm the marshmallow thief."

With that comment, his peers broke into laughter.

He said, "It was just a joke. I didn't know it was going to create such a mess. I just thought it would be funny."

"It was funny, all right. Try to get my group of ninth graders to laugh with you as they sit at their desks and work instead of getting to make this project. See how funny it is then."

Realizing the time, I told the students that they had about nine more minutes left in class, and to return to their labs to try to complete their treats. This applied to everyone except Dana and Chip. I told them I needed to meet with them to discuss their punishment.

While the class filed back into the kitchen, I began to discuss this episode further with the two students. I wanted them to know I admired them for coming forth and admitting their mistake. On the other hand, I wanted them to learn a great lesson from this that would stick with them for the rest of their lives. I wanted them to see how closely this episode resembled other facets of life by showing the consequences for breaking rules, especially when tampering with another's property.

"You will need to write a two-page report explaining the details of this incident, including the reasons why you should have chosen not to do this mischievous act. Feel free to add any additional comments you deem necessary to relate the happenings of this event. This is due tomorrow at 7:20 a.m. and you also will serve two morning detentions. Please be in my room promptly at 7:20 with report in hand, and be ready to stay until the first bell. If you do not show up, I will send an office referral immediately. Do you understand? Do you feel this is a fair deal?"

"Yes," replied Dana, "I can't believe I'm having to do this, but I see your reasoning. I just didn't think it would cause such a mess."

"I didn't either," Chip chimed in. Laughing, he said, "It was just a bag of marshmallows. I'll pay you back," as he pulled out his billfold to retrieve a dollar.

"That's not the point, Chip. I've already given my explanation and it is a waste of time to stand here and rehash what has been discussed. You made a mistake. Now accept responsibility, complete the assignment, and wash your hands clean of this whole thing."

"If I don't do it, what's gonna happen? I'm eighteen, you know. Are they gonna take me to jail and lock me up? I can just see myself getting booked and somebody asking, 'What are you in for, buddy?'

"The ultimate Christmas crime: I'm a marshmallow thief.

"C'mon, this is ridiculous, Miss Ledford."

"Ridiculous or not, you have been given a choice. I hope you choose to complete the paper. I think it would make for some interesting reading."

As the class came to a close, the students eagerly rushed into the halls to begin tales of juicy gossip about The Marshmallow Thief. As Chip and Dana left the room, I hollered, "What's it going to be, Chip?"

He turned, with somewhat of an embarrassed look, and mumbled, "I'll see you in the morning."

I told this story to drive home a couple of important points about teaching. Fridays are hectic—for students, teachers, and even members of the administration.

There are probably more behavior problems on Fridays than on any other day. Everyone has his or her mind on the weekend, and we all just try to get through till the final bell sounds. It's a struggle to keep kids focused, so projects or rewards are usually offered on Fridays to help ease some of the tension and help the clock tick just a bit faster.

But rules must remain strongly intact on Fridays, just as on any other day of the week. It is crucial that discipline be enforced, especially on Fridays, so the learning process can continue to take place. It is vital that new teachers learn this consistency quickly, and sometimes this is a tough thing to accomplish, as the above story illustrates.

Sometimes it takes drastic measures, such as making the entire class sit down, to get the kids' attention. I firmly believe in individualized discipline, but there are exceptions to this rule when you don't know who the troublemaker is. Luckily, the behavioral management technique I chose to use in this situation worked.

Teachers should be required to wear TGIF buttons on Fridays. I think the kids would love it (and the teachers, too). It would be like wearing pep ribbons for the home football games ... an outward sign of enthusiasm and spirit for the upcoming weekend could be a real morale booster.

Teachers really need to think more seriously about the TGIF motto. We need to enjoy ourselves, relax, and take a true break from the hectic workweek.

I find this difficult to do. I tend to be an obsessive-compulsive individual, very much a perfectionist. It is hard for me to relax, even on the weekends, due to my drive to achieve, do, and create more ideas and innovations.

Professional educators need to look forward to the weekends, to getting away from the weeklong rat race of ball games, meetings, lesson planning, parent-teacher conferences and grading of papers.

We deserve a break. TGIF!

rinted with permission from Bruce Plante.

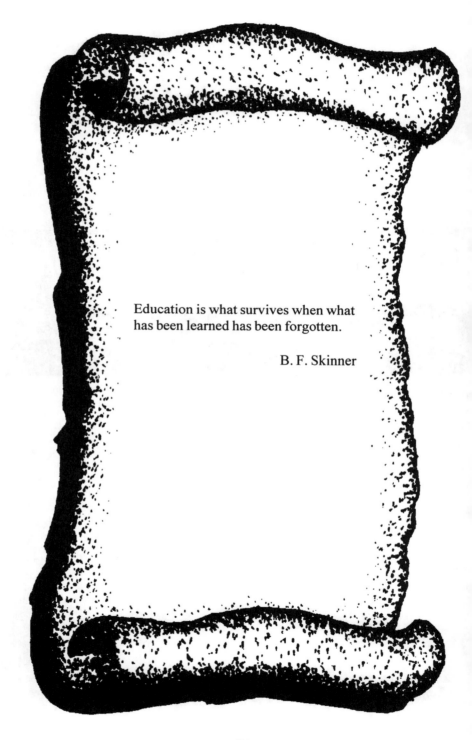

Education is what survives when what
has been learned has been forgotten.

B. F. Skinner

Is It Monday Already?

12

As I rolled over from a good night's sleep, I glanced at the clock and couldn't believe what I saw. Big, block, digital numbers stared me directly in the eyes: 7:15.

How could I have overslept? Did my alarm clock not go off? Did I accidentally turn it off in my sleep? What happened? I was panic stricken. My heart raced. I broke out into a cold sweat, for fear of being late sent cold chills up my spine.

I leaped into the shower to wake myself up from this nightmare, only to find out that it was reality. It was Monday and I was going to be late to work for the first time.

As I hurriedly threw my contacts in and brushed my teeth, I began to think about my day. "Oh, no, today is faculty meeting—how could I have forgotten?"

Looking down at my watch I became upset when I realized the meeting started in only twenty short minutes. There is no way I can make it across the mountain in time, I thought as I wondered what my principal would think of me.

On top of it all it was raining outside, which meant I would have to reduce my speed for safe driving conditions, adding an additional five to seven minutes to my trip. I'll be lucky even to get there on time for school, I thought.

As I ran out of the house in a frenzy, I felt out of sorts to be in such a predicament. I felt as if my professionalism had plummeted as I rolled down the windows to dry my hair with my "455 blowdryer" (four windows down at 55 mph). I looked like a wreck, felt like a wreck, and just prayed I would not have a wreck. I lived for the moment I would arrive safely at school.

As I topped the mountain, I saw cars ahead—and they weren't moving. Road construction signs began to appear and then all of a sudden I was at a standstill.

"It has to be Monday," I said to myself aloud, over the radio. "This would never be happening on any other day except Monday— I hate Mondays!"

My tension level rose.

Realizing I would definitely miss the faculty meeting, I decided to call the school and explain that I would be late (cellular phones are a must for teachers, especially females, and I urge every individual to invest in one). Having to make this call was ripping out my heart—it was a much-dreaded call for a first-year teacher to have to make.

"Hello, Whiteville High School," came over the line in a feminine voice.

"Is this Edna?"

"Yes, it is."

"Edna, this is Jada. Would you please inform Mr. Shipley that I am running behind this morning? At this point, I'm on top of the mountain stuck in traffic at the construction site. I didn't even know they were planning to do this. I'm very frustrated and it's inevitable that I will be late."

"Well, I'll tell him, Jada, however, he's in the faculty meeting right now," she replied.

"Oh well. I had hoped I would catch him before the meeting. Anyway, please be sure and tell him I called."

After I hung up, I felt worse than ever. Did I really expect my principal to believe this story? And now that I think about it, why should he?

I wheeled into the school parking lot at 7:45 Central Time (8:45 my time), exactly five minutes before my first period class would begin. I jogged to the building, signed in and went to find Mr. Shipley. As I rounded the entrance into his office, he met me with a "where have you been?" look on his face.

"Did Edna tell you I called?"

"No, I haven't talked with her."

Great, just great, I thought.

"I've been in traffic on the mountain. I'm very sorry I missed the faculty meeting. This was definitely a professional error on my part and I'll do whatever it takes to correct it."

"I'll meet with all those who missed the meeting immediately after school or tomorrow during your planning period to discuss the details of the meeting."

"Again, I apologize. I'll see you after school."

After his words of encouragement that everything was OK and that he appreciated my call, I turned and rushed to make it to my class before the tardy bell rang.

The above situation is one I hoped would never occur again. Mondays bring on such a load of unexpected events that sometimes it even scares the teacher. But from this episode I learned three very important lessons I think all teachers should follow (or any other employee for that matter).

First, if you see that you are going to be late, call and let your employer know ahead of time. This can help reduce administration and student anxiety. Even though the message had not been relayed to Mr. Shipley, he would have found out sooner or later that I had contacted the school. This shows an employer you are thinking ahead and are concerned about keeping open communication lines.

Secondly, I learned that honesty is the best, and should be the only, policy. If a mistake is made, readily admit it, endure the consequences, put it behind you and move forward. Employers view honesty as an admirable trait that builds strong character. Don't get caught telling "little white lies."

And lastly, go immediately to the principal, if available, or to the highest official and speak one-on-one about your problems. Sending a message by a student or another teacher does not serve as a substitute for a personal confrontation. Even though it may seem a bit uncomfortable, it is the best workable choice.

Mondays come and go, always signaling the beginning of another week. It is so important for a true professional to put all the uneventful things behind him or her and rise to the call of duty to perform at his or her peak once again.

It's crucial to be viewed as an optimist rather than a pessimist by your students. Make it a high priority to be a confident, cheerful kind of instructor. I promise you the attitude presented by the teacher on Monday morning shapes the students' outlook for the week.

Mondays must be handled differently than any other day of the week. If any class has to have energy and power, it must be on Monday. Kids are still sleepy from the weekend, thinking about the weekend, wanting to share news about the weekend, and the last place they want to be is in my class listening to my lecture.

I have found that using icebreakers on Mondays, to get the kids up and involved, is a great way to start the class. Competitions for prizes (even if it's a piece of three-cent bubble gum) have a way of motivating students. Even a review game of some kind would be challenging and get the students refocused after the distractions of the weekend.

Because I feel so strongly that Monday is a special day, I never (or almost never) give tests that day. I have found test scores to be significantly lower. As much as it seems logical that students would have three nights and two full days to prepare for an exam, that just doesn't happen. Even if a kid, heaven forbid, remembers to take his or her notebook home to study, it usually stays in one place until picked up again for school on Monday.

Kids choose to do other things on the weekend; they play or do work they have to do or want to do. And not only kids, but teachers, too. We pack our bags or briefcases full of papers to grade, projects to read through, lessons to plan, and materials to review only to expend the energy required to carry this load to and from the car and then back to the school. What a waste of time and energy it seems, but we have all fallen victim to this vicious cycle at one time or another.

So let's face it. Teachers and students like to procrastinate. Knowing this, I feel better testing my kids on Tuesday through Thursday, and, with some exceptions, on Friday. You run into the same situation Friday as on Monday, but kids will vote every time that Fridays beat Mondays, hands down.

inted with permission from Bruce Plante.

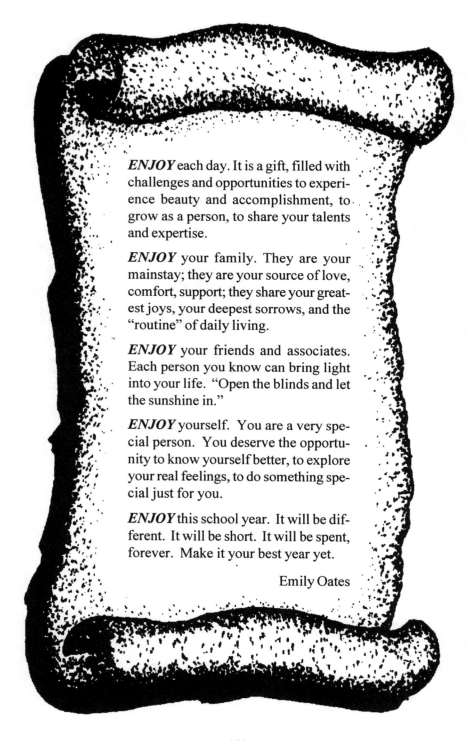

ENJOY each day. It is a gift, filled with challenges and opportunities to experience beauty and accomplishment, to grow as a person, to share your talents and expertise.

ENJOY your family. They are your mainstay; they are your source of love, comfort, support; they share your greatest joys, your deepest sorrows, and the "routine" of daily living.

ENJOY your friends and associates. Each person you know can bring light into your life. "Open the blinds and let the sunshine in."

ENJOY yourself. You are a very special person. You deserve the opportunity to know yourself better, to explore your real feelings, to do something special just for you.

ENJOY this school year. It will be different. It will be short. It will be spent, forever. Make it your best year yet.

Emily Oates

Thirteen Blind Mice | **13**

I was lucky this year. My school provided wonderful facilities. Some teachers are not so lucky, or should I say most teachers do not enjoy this luxury as a first-year teacher. However, there will always be room for improvement.

As I toured my school, I was pleasantly surprised at the condition it was in. Carpet lined the halls, brightly painted lockers sported the Tiger logo, classrooms had freshly painted walls, and the bathrooms were free of graffiti. What more could one ask for?

The home economics department was fabulous—a large, spacious room with three distinct areas for work: a lecture area with a chalkboard, teacher desk and the students' work tables, the well-kept kitchen facility with cooking labs designed for the foods and nutrition unit, and the large group area with dining table, open flow space for projects and sewing machines. As a bonus, in the back of the room was a storage and toiletry section for my personal use.

On the surface it seemed as though I had everything a first-year teacher could dream of. The room was in a wreck, but I was sure it would all be put back together before school started. But it was only a few months later that I found some problems.

I went to the school several days before the onset of student activity to clear the room, inventory the kitchen and file materials. Boy, what a job I had to do! As I rummaged through the cabinets, I found remnants of old food, baking sheets with cookie crumbs on them, and opened containers of sugar and spices.

I hope this is not how the students treat the food labs, I thought to myself as I emptied out the cabinets, washed them down with bleach and sprayed disinfectant.

"It's a miracle the mice haven't carried this room off," I mumbled as I continued to work.

After I had the kitchen in somewhat satisfactory condition, I made my way to the back storage section of the room. Books, posters, supplies, projects—you name it, it was crammed into or, I might say, thrown into this small area.

I'm sure there were lots of other surprises to be found, but I didn't dare go digging any further. I somehow managed to move stuff back and forth as I needed it so I could delay clearing the junk out.

As the school year progressed, I began to smell an odor whenever I was in the back retrieving textbooks or supplies. I kept saying to myself, "something must be rotten back here," because the smell worsened as the days passed by.

Later I decided to brave the much-delayed job and tackle it head-on. I asked my vocational assistant to come in during fourth period (my planning time) and help me. She agreed to come and help get everything organized.

"Gross" could be heard echoing through the room as Cathy and I pulled items from the piles of rubbish. The smell was getting stronger, much stronger, so we knew we were getting close to the problem. And did we ever find it, or, I should say, them.

Yuck! Dead mice. One, no, two dead mice were rotting on top of old manuals in a box that had mildewed. We found a third one as we cleaned out a box of plastic babies used for demonstrations in child development.

A job I first thought would take an hour turned into a week-long project of sorting, discarding and disinfecting. We finally had the area cleaned up and organized for easy accessibility.

Just to be on the safe side, I asked Cathy to get some rat traps from the janitor to place in various spots around the room. Our janitor sent word back that they did not have rat traps, but they did have a device called a "rat board" that was supposed to be far more effective than the traps.

When the janitor brought some down to me, I laughed and said, "Are you kidding me? Do you think I'm going to waste my time with these things? I'll go to the store tonight and buy some real rat traps."

"Well, you might ought to try these tonight and see how they work, you never know."

"OK, but how do they work, anyway?"

"Just pull this piece of paper off the board to expose the very sticky surface—and I mean it is sticky, so try not to get it on your hands, it's hard to get off—then lay them on the floor or countertops you might expect a mouse to travel across. The sweet, sugary aroma will attract the mice to it, and if they make contact with the board they're not going anywhere!"

"You mean they will lie there and squeal till they die?"

"You guessed it. You'll have to come in and fold the boards over and dispose of them."

"Yeah, right! I don't think I'll have to worry about that. It pretty much looks like a cheap rip-off type product to me. But what the heck, I'll give it a try."

To be honest, I had so much on my mind the next morning that I had forgotten all about the mice until I opened my door and flipped on the lights. I rushed over to the kitchen in a state of shock, for I could not believe my eyes.

Every rat board had a mouse on it, and one had two. I ran to get Opal (the janitor) so she could see it, and also to admit what a fool I had made of myself by doubting that the boards would actually work.

We captured thirteen mice in all: thirteen little, dumb, blind mice that walked right into the traps without even knowing they were there. I was overwhelmed at the outcome, to put it mildly, but glad to have a mice-free room at last.

Well, I thought the mice were gone. A few days later, while in the middle of a very important lecture, a student squealed "a mouse!" As the class totally lost its train of thought (several girls even jumped up into their seats), I realized our problems were not over.

But I was more disturbed by the distraction one little tiny mouse could cause. One mouse can distract a child's mind for the next forty minutes (or the remainder of the class period) and he or she will probably go into the hall talking about what had just happened, thus distracting the next class. Then this same kid, or group of kids, comes into class the next day fearing a similar experience, resulting in another completely wasted class period.

How can this be prevented? I put this responsibility primarily on the school system. Schools need to do a much better job at maintaining a rodent- and pest-free environment.

Kids are distracted by these things and have every right to be, just as any consumer is nauseated at the sight of a roach crawling up the wall while they are trying to enjoy a nice evening meal. It is repulsive and gives the feeling of unclean, unhealthy and just plain unsanitary conditions. There is no excuse for this in a public school system, especially not in the home economics department.

But teachers have to contend with these less-than-desirable circum- stances we find ourselves in from time to time. And we just have to do the best we can with what we have, while continuing to push for improvements to be made.

Speaking of improvements, I encountered other problems that year that were never remedied. For instance, I had an oven that didn't work when I was first hired, so I reported it to be fixed. Even after calling (and calling, and calling), the request was never granted.

This put an added stress on food lab preparation. Due to the limited equipment, labs had to carry-over extra days and were sometimes even can- celed. Having difficulty getting equipment serviced or repaired was just an- other one of the surprises I had to deal with.

Looking back on my first year, I think I kind of resembled those thir- teen little blind mice, as I like to call them. I felt I was a useless little crea- ture scurrying around the school, getting into whatever I could find. I also felt like I had blinders on because I couldn't seem to predict what was ahead. And then I felt trapped for most of the year, because I realized that as a first-year teacher I couldn't do or say much of anything that would really have any weight to change some of these problems.

I guess I can just be thankful I never stopped squealing long enough for someone to think I was dead and dispose of me.

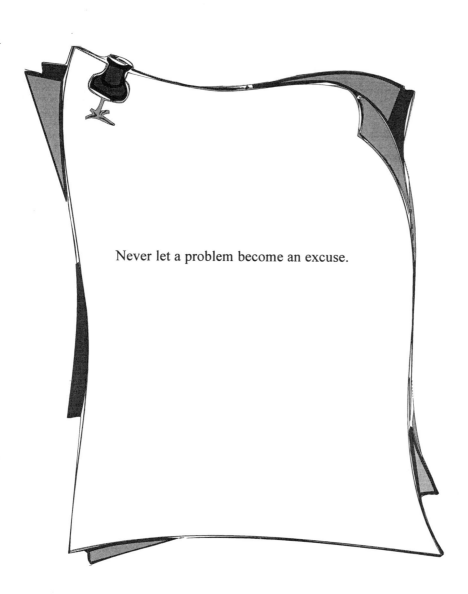

Never let a problem become an excuse.

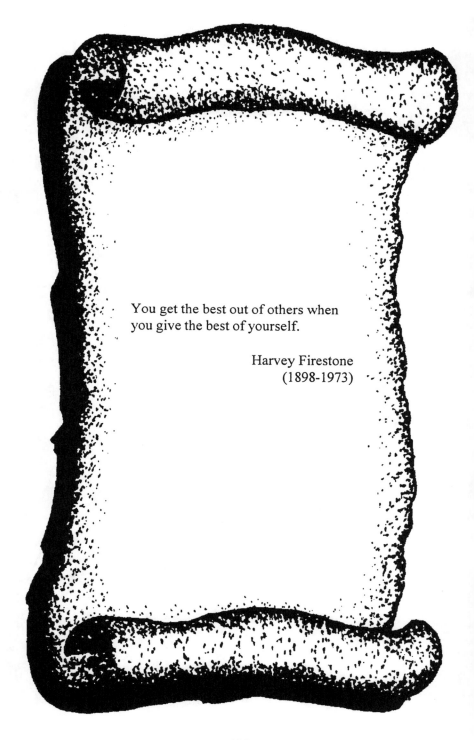

You get the best out of others when
you give the best of yourself.

Harvey Firestone
(1898-1973)

Boosting Kids Self-Esteem

14

As the kids filled the auditorium, you could feel tension racing among certain students. It was the Seventh Annual Awards Day at Whiteville High School, and a few select individuals would soon be recognized in front of their friends for academic excellence. A faculty representative from each department was on stage to announce awards for programs in the 1992-93 school term.

I knew a secret most did not know. It was a secret I couldn't wait to tell, as I was eagerly anticipating the students' response. As it came closer to time to announce my award, my excitement grew.

"And now, Jada Ledford."

My time had finally arrived. Walking to the podium with a big smile on my face, I caught the students' attention. As I glanced out in the audience to see if Justin was there, he was laughing with his friends and having a good time. We made eye contact, and at that point I think he knew something was up.

"It is my pleasure to announce this year's winner of the Home Economics Academic Award. This student is very deserving, as he— yes, I said he; Home Ec's not just for girls anymore—maintained a 99.6 average throughout the year. This person has worked very hard, and at this time I would like to congratulate Justin Sanders as this year's winner."

Boy, was this news to the student body. As Justin tried to make his way up to the stage, his male friends exchanged high fives and cheered him on.

Even though I'm sure Justin was a bit embarrassed, since it is such an uncommon occurrence for a boy to excel in home economics, he was enjoying the attention. He was grinning from ear to ear, and you could just tell his self-esteem had been heightened as he received his award while his peers and other teachers applauded him.

I tell this simple story to show you that kids usually respond favorably to recognition. Students love to be honored in front of their friends and family for their achievements. Taking the time to recognize students during awards day or hosting awards banquets is vitally important in developing high self-esteem levels in teenagers.

There are a vast number of ways to encourage young people and make them feel good about themselves. During my first year of teaching, I tried several techniques and would like to share some of the ones the kids really enjoyed.

1. ***Bulletin Boards.*** I developed a bulletin board titled, "What's Happening?" in my classroom to display student involvement in the school. I would take photos of class activities and post them on the board, cut out newspaper clippings when my students made the paper for sports or scholarships, post humorous comic strips relative to the lives of high school kids, and any other interesting pieces of information that I could find.

    The kids really enjoyed rushing into class and seeing what new events were happening that I had put up on the board. They loved the idea and it proved to be fun and exciting for everyone.

2. ***Games.*** As a teacher, I always have my eyes open when shopping for neat little prizes and gifts for students. There is nothing better than receiving an award or a prize for achievements. Kids love contests because they thrive on competition.

A great game that kids love to play is review bingo. You distribute pre-made bingo cards with chips and put your vocabulary or terms that have been studied on the board or overhead projector. Have the students randomly pick a term for each box on their card. Give each one the free space in the middle and begin the game.

I usually like to start out with the traditional "straight line" bingo. The first student to cover a straight line in any direction wins that game. I begin to call out the definitions of the words or terms, and if the student knows the term they place a marker over that space.

We continue the game until a student screams "BINGO," at which point I check to make sure the terms are correct. After a winner is confirmed, I award a prize (usually candy) and then the kids beg to hurry to get started on the next game. You can continue playing with the same card and play "T" bingo, "X" bingo, or "Full Card" bingo. This game has proved very successful as a review and as a way for the kids to have fun studying.

Other competitions that kids of all ages enjoy are puzzles, scrambled words and brain teasers. Every so often, make up a sheet of scrambled terms or crossword puzzles about the unit you are studying and award prizes for those who finish first.

Believe it or not, kids love stickers, even the big kids. Buy a set of scratch-n-sniff stickers or stars to award for finishing first.

Trivia is another thing that kids thrive on. We play a game called Not So Trivial that is geared for Vocational Home Economics courses. It is much like Trivial Pursuit, but the questions come from categories such as Family and Interpersonal Relationships, Foods and Nutrition, Child Development, Clothing and Textiles, Housing and Interiors, and Consumer Issues.

I divide the students into teams and play rounds to see who can complete each category first. The winning team is usually awarded a homework pass, which can be used at any time in place of the assigned homework for a 100 grade.

3. *Giveaways.* I like to set up incentives for perfect attendance and highest grades from time to time. Each semester you can

run a long-term contest for each of these areas and award a prize. Students love T-shirts, but that can get rather expensive. Get out into the community and call on the locals to donate or sponsor your class contests. You'll be surprised at what you'll get.

Also, it's a lot of fun to keep kids on their toes, so I occasionally offer a random door prize. Be creative and think of a neat way to give an unexpected prize (for example, put a sticker under a student's seat, put a number on the board and pass around a box of numbers for the kids to choose from, and whoever chooses the proper number wins). The main idea here is to keep kids guessing about what you are going to do next. Stay in control, but have fun doing it.

By the way, I almost forgot. Give treats on special occasions. High school students genuinely appreciate this sort of thing. Each of the major holidays is a nice opportunity to do this. Students especially love heart suckers on Valentines!

4.   *Sports.* Your students want to see you at ball games. I realize it's very difficult to go to all the sporting events offered at the high school level, but pick out a game or two each season and be there for your kids.

It thrills me to watch their reactions when they see their teachers in attendance. This is such a morale booster, because for a lot of high school kids sports is the one thing that keeps them involved in school. And always follow up the next school day by making a positive comment about his or her playing time.

5.   *Verbal Attention.* Kids don't always have to have a tangible item to feel appreciated. Verbal praise and appreciation are one of the best ways to turn a kid's attitude completely around. Just by calling kids by their given names makes them feel important in your class.

As I mentioned earlier, I make it a point to learn all of my students' names at the beginning of the year. Make this a high priority, whether you are a new teacher or a veteran. Kids respond much more favorably when called upon in a respectful manner, using their proper names. Also make a strong effort to honor kids verbally, so their peers can hear. After the officer elections for a club you sponsor, give those kids recognition in daily announcements. Big dividends will be paid over and over again for this type of attention.

6. *Role-Playing.* Even though this may take extra planning time, role-playing in the classroom can be a vital tool. Students will do a much better job of internalizing the material if given the opportunity to act it out and make it come alive.

This is not for all students, so it might be best only to take volunteers for an activity of this nature. However, you will be amazed at how much students can draw from this, even if they are not actively participating.

Be sure to always have a follow-up discussion regarding the roles that have just been played. This creates an open atmosphere for students to communicate their true feelings on the subject.

7. *Responsibility.* Give kids responsibility whenever it is possible to work it in. Make kids accountable for their actions and reactions to others.

Children like to feel that you believe in them. Give them the opportunity to prove responsibility in the classroom and always recognize them if success is seen.

8. *Success.* All students, and people in general, need to experience success in life. As challenging as it may be, we as educators need to find ways for our underachievers to be successful.

Try to allot a certain portion of each class one day each week to an activity or project everyone can master. What a difference it can make in the life of a child when they feel capable!

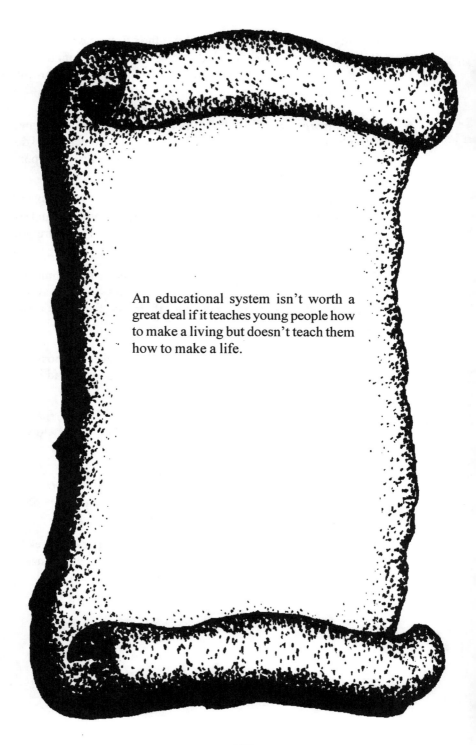

An educational system isn't worth a great deal if it teaches young people how to make a living but doesn't teach them how to make a life.

What the Heck is Home Ec?

15

While introducing myself and making small talk with several people at a school parent-teacher conference one day, a woman candidly spoke up and said, "I don't think I've had the opportunity to meet you. You must be a new teacher."

"Yes ma'am, I am. I'm the new home economics teacher and assistant girls basketball coach."

Laughing, she said, "Well, I have a son who's in high school, but I'm sure he won't be taking home economics because he's going to college."

Whether she meant that to be an insult or not, I offered a quick rebuttal.

"Then he needs it most! It is a class of life skills; skills needed to make it in life after high school.

"I think you may be misinformed on what is being taught today in home economics. The integration of boys into the program has increased most classes to 40 percent male. It is so important for both sexes because they may find themselves a single parent raising a child, living on their own, preparing meals, living on a budget, building, designing, decorating or caring for a home.

"The need is ever-so-great to reverse the thinking that home economics is an all-girls course of cooking and sewing that only non-college-bound kids take. It is not a crip course for lower achievers so they can raise their GPA. It is a sound, hands-on, academic-based class for students of all achievement levels."

From the look in this woman's eye I knew that I had given her more than she bargained for. I think she was jolted by my response, and a bit shocked that I was so prepared to reply to such comments.

She never gave a reply. I'm still not sure if she was just at a loss for words, if she didn't want to go on with the conversation, or if she realized she had made a statement out of ignorance and wished she could take it back. For some reason I think it was the latter, or at least I hope so, but this was an experience I was sure she would not forget any time soon.

Attitudes of this type toward home economics are very common. Most people are misinformed and uneducated about what is actually taught in vocational home economics courses. Because of this problem, I hope the following information proves to be useful in explaining what home economic programs are all about.

Vocational home economics education prepares youth for competencies in personal and family life, the work of the family, and for occupations based on home economics knowledge and skills.

The focus is the family and the belief that the well-being of our society is based on the social and economic well-being of families. Families are viewed as the primary source of human fulfillment in terms of love, security and acceptance. Fundamental to vocational home economics instruction is the relationship that exists between a quality home and family life and a productive, satisfying work life.

Home economics consumer and homemaking programs promote a healthy family life and aim to help prevent problems related to family instability, child abuse, substance abuse, inadequate nutrition and resource management.

Home economics-related occupational education concentrates on employability in the work place.

A unique feature of home economics education is its potential for addressing individual, family and societal problems and applying home economics knowledge to problems that relate to life in today's or tomorrow's world.

The ultimate goal of home economics education is to strengthen the quality of home, work, and family life by providing the opportunity for adolescents to gain knowledge and skills essential to become effective contributors to home and society.

The broad objectives for vocational home economics education are to enable students to:

1. Establish and maintain effective, well-functioning families and homes that promote self-understanding and foster the development of individuals;

2. Solve problems involving nurturing human development, feeding, clothing, housing people and managing resources to satisfy needs;

3. Understand how to manage the multiple roles they will face throughout life;

4. Evaluate and accommodate economic, social, political and technological changes influencing the family;

5. Choose to live intelligently, promote individual and family health, make wise decisions, contribute to the social-economic setting and instill individual well-being in both home and work;

6. To prepare males and females to become employable as they assume the roles of homemaker or wage earner;

7. Develop leadership abilities through participation in FHA (Future Homemakers of America) or Home Economics-Related Occupations; and

8. Prepare for professional leadership in home economics areas (*Home Economics Curriculum*, 1990).

Many issues featured on the evening news are also discussion topics in home economics classes. These include family values, race relations, AIDS, drug and alcohol abuse, illiteracy, housing, quality child care, the environment, teen pregnancy, the elderly, financial management, abortion and adoption, divorce, violence, crime, the economy, taxes, sexual equality, teen suicide, adequate nutrition, single parenting and child abuse.

Along with home economics also comes a youth organization titled FHA. So, what exactly is a homemaker?

A homemaker is anyone who contributes to his or her own well-being and the well-being of the persons they live with. If you clean the yard, take care of your sister, write to your grandmother, call your brother on his birthday, help your dad find a good second-hand car, cook dinner for the family or do the grocery shopping, you are a homemaker.

If you take care of your health, try to look your best, deal with peer pressure, have fun with your friends, make good consumer decisions, get involved in making decisions at school or work at home, you are a homemaker.

And if FHA was interesting enough to attract star athletes Herschel Walker and Bo Jackson as members, maybe it can work for you!

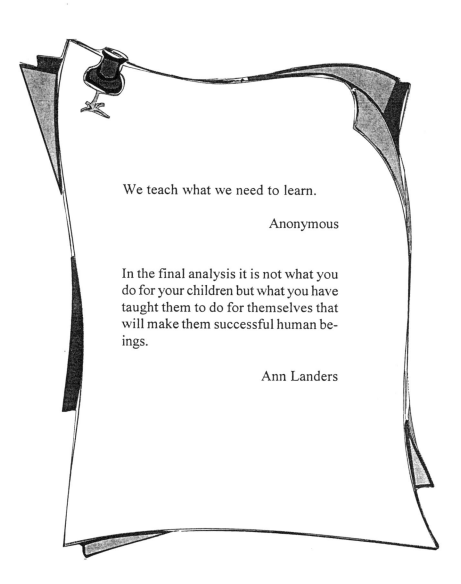

We teach what we need to learn.

Anonymous

In the final analysis it is not what you do for your children but what you have taught them to do for themselves that will make them successful human beings.

Ann Landers

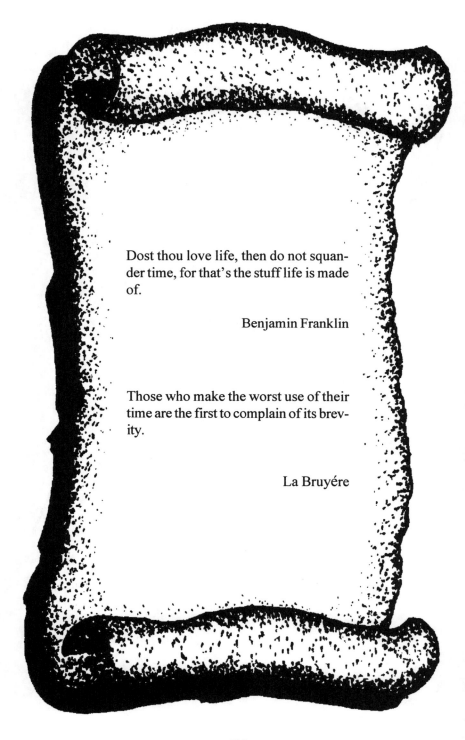

Dost thou love life, then do not squander time, for that's the stuff life is made of.

Benjamin Franklin

Those who make the worst use of their time are the first to complain of its brevity.

La Bruyére

Make the Most
of Your Minutes

16

"To Do" List

✓ Pick up dry cleaning (I have hardly anything left to wear)

✓ Get trash bags (the trash is mounting and I must get it bagged up tonight)

✓ Try to find time to clean the house (it looks like a bomb went off and sent things flying everywhere)

✓ Go out on a real date with Kevin (somewhere besides Waffle House)

✓ Make out unit test for Child Development (surely those kids have learned this material by now)

✓ Paint my nails (heaven forbid I pamper myself)

✓ Get in bed before 1:00 a.m. (I've got to get more sleep!)

With a "To Do" list packed with more things than I could possibly do, I suddenly realized time management is one of the most important skills to master in order to be a successful teacher. Being able to allot certain amounts of time for certain types of activities is a must if you want to get everything accomplished, and "To Do" lists are the only method I found that worked for me during this hectic year.

Lists serve as an outline or a guide for my day. I am careful to make a new list each night for the upcoming day's events. Then as I complete each task I mark through it so I can move on to the next item. The feeling of satisfaction as I check them off is therapy for me.

Each of us must find time in our busy schedules to plan. Planning takes time, but saves precious time in the future. Making "To Do" lists helps to structure time and allows a person to function from an organized perspective. I have found being organized not only is impressive to your students, other faculty members and administrators, but is a must if you want to maintain a sense of professionalism and keep your sanity.

We also must define goals. Setting long- and short-term goals gives us direction in life. It prioritizes our time and allows us to focus on what lies ahead. Not only do we need to set goals, but we need to remind ourselves of them.

I have found it beneficial to post goals in places where I cannot miss seeing them, perhaps on a filing cabinet or even at my desk. It is important to review them often. Visualize reaching your goals and the satisfaction you will feel when they are accomplished.

Developing a filing system is mandatory for the first-year teacher. I started some files at the onset of school and organized each subject I would be teaching. Proper labeling and adequate space is essential to good filing.

This takes time, sometimes more time than you really have to devote to it. But hang on—be patient until the bulk of the project is finished. You will be so glad throughout the year, because good filing is the secret to saving time. It becomes easy to retrieve items that once took hours to find.

And, do not forget, filing is an ongoing project. Always feel free to add to your files or take things away as the year progresses.

Save newspaper clippings of articles that directly tie into your program so you can have them available for use in the classroom. Kids like to see that what they are learning is directly related to what is actually happening in our present society. It is the teacher's responsibility to make that connection, and you will find it rewarding to see how eager kids will be to help you find newspaper articles for future study.

I could continue for pages on what I think to be the best ways to make the most of your minutes. But I think this list of twelve time management tips that I was given while attending a leadership conference will be a more concise way of getting my point across:

1. Do not postpone getting started.

2. Do a job with zest.

3. Make use of odd moments.

4. Learn to conserve time.

5. Place tasks in priority order.

6. Group similar tasks.

7. Delegate responsibilities to others.

8. Practice dovetailing.

9. Simplify jobs and eliminate steps.

10. Establish a routine.

11. Give yourself deadlines and meet them.

12. Execute your plan. There comes a time when you just have to produce.

Even with all the planning and organizing there are still some things that keep you from making the most of your minutes, and those are called time wasters. Everyone is familiar with his own hang-ups, or areas where he gets bogged down. However, see if you can relate to the list (on the following page) of time wasters I became acquainted with while attending a workshop.

As I reviewed this list, I saw myself wasting time in many of these areas. It is easy to get so caught up in what you're doing that you don't have time to get the job done. It is also convenient to fall into some of these time wasters.

For example, my planning time was fourth period. In the beginning, I thought this was great. A good, clean break in the middle of the day would fit perfectly into my lunch schedule. I would not have to inhale my food in twenty-five minutes. I could relax and enjoy it.

That is exactly what I did.

Internal Time Wasters	External Time Wasters
Trying to do too much at once	Incomplete information
Unrealistic time estimates	Telephone
Procrastinating	Television
Lack of organization	Routine tasks
Failure to listen	Lunch, dinner, "eating times"
Trying to do it all by myself	Interruptions
Unable to say "no"	Meetings
Refusal to let others do the job	Lack of priorities
Trying to involve everyone	Attention to too many people
Making snappy decisions	Outside activities
Blaming others	Poor communication
Personal and outside activities	Mistakes (especially unnecessary ones)

I began to spend a portion of my planning time taking an extended lunch. It was hard to break away from the relaxing atmosphere of sitting and chatting with my peers, and time would slip away before I even realized it. Sometimes I would find myself spending fifteen to twenty extra minutes talking with faculty and students during lunch. What an external time waster!

If you are a teacher reading this book you know what an awful habit this is to break. But a good lesson can be learned from this. Adults enjoy lunch and other social times with our friends just like the kids do. If the kids knew they could either stay in lunch an extra fifteen minutes or go to a quiet study hall and get a few bonus minutes of study time, which option do you think nine out of ten would choose?

This brings up another good point.

You need to try and stay open-minded and focused when teaching kids about making proper use of time. Do not be a "do as I say, not as I do" type of teacher. Make it apparent by your example that you are conscious of time, and your students will be more likely to follow your lead.

Also, you might want to try using students who finish their work early to help with certain tasks such as stapling papers, changing bulletin boards or filing. This can build confidence and help develop maturity, while instilling in them the importance of making every minute count.

I learned a very good lesson my first year. I must give myself specific amounts of time to accomplish tasks, because I fare better when given deadlines. As Lee College President Paul Conn said at a writing seminar, "Set deadlines you will hate yourself for." And I did just that.

I had to commit myself to taking only twenty-five minutes for lunch and returning to the room for planning. If I had not done this early on, I am not sure I could ever have broken myself from this major time waster.

Lastly, one thing that I tried to do is reward myself for getting things done. Just as students need to see success and feel they have accomplished something, so do we.

Occasionally, when the last item on the "To Do" list is checked off, treat yourself. I find this to be a time of renewal to reflect on the fruits of my labor. A nice, hot bubble bath topped off with a good book, or an evening out to dinner, or maybe a shopping splurge (my favorite choice, by far) is a great way to pamper myself for seeing a job through to the end.

Believe me, the benefits of such rewards go a long, long way.

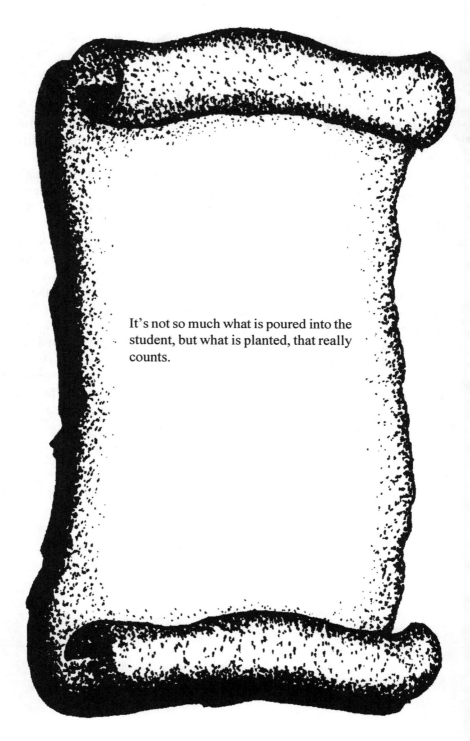

It's not so much what is poured into the student, but what is planted, that really counts.

Traveling Tidbits | **17**

On the morning of March 13, 1993, I awoke to an event Chattanooga had not witnessed in more than 100 years. It was pure white, soft and fluffy, twenty-two inches deep, and covered every inch of outdoor space. I was shocked by its beauty, but even more shocked that the local weather anchors were finally right in their predictions.

The "Snow Storm of '93" was here.

This massive snowstorm closed schoolhouse doors across the area. Television news updates anxiously reported all the details of this great happening. Not only were schools closed, but so were stores and businesses of every kind, and most roads were impassable. Our world came to a halt as we watched the oversized flakes fall.

I was ecstatic! What could be more exciting than to be out of school and forced to enjoy this natural beauty? The answer quickly came to me: I was supposed to be flying out of Nashville, heading to sunny 90-degree Trinidad, in only three short days.

Spring break would begin on Monday and I was going to Trinidad to be a short-term volunteer missionary. I would take personal leave days for the second week to finish my mission project. I would be ministering to many children and teaching them about American sports.

As I gazed out my window, I suddenly wanted all the snow to go away. I had spent numerous hours in preparation and countless dollars to finance the trip—money that I, along with others, had invested, but which at this point would be nonrefundable. I must make my trip, I thought to myself. I must have the opportunity to teach these children who are eagerly awaiting our arrival.

I began to wonder what some of my students were thinking. Some had questioned my reasons for going and were quite curious about the trip.

"Why would you want to give up your spring break, Miss Ledford, to go be with more kids, trying to teach them things, when you could be in Florida, lying on the beach? You deserve a break. Why would you do that?"

Such questions and comments were an everyday occurrence after I explained to the students I would be gone. They really did not understand my reasons for going, and that was OK, but I was going to attempt to explain why my heart was so involved with mission work of this kind.

"I will agree with you. I think I do need a break. However, I long to help and work with kids of all kinds, regardless of color, race or religion. I love kids, believe it or not, and am even willing to spend my vacation days with them.

"Furthermore, traveling does so much for an individual. It expands the mind and soul like nothing else. It develops one's character and sense of compassion on an international level. It allows a person to step into the lives of those who are totally different from our culture, and to live and function in their world for a period of time. It has a way of erasing or reducing prejudice and bias we may have toward a given people.

"All of this," I said, "produces a deep sense of satisfaction for me, as I'm sure it does for others. It broadens my teaching range. I will be a better teacher when I return, just wait and see."

As my students listened intently, I could still see disbelief in their eyes. Most of these kids had never traveled 50 miles, much less 2,000 miles. This was totally above their heads.

Trying to convince these kids that education is an international concern, and that teachers are committed to giving more of themselves than required, was like trying to get them to see the importance of Algebra II and trigonometry in their lives. They could not see the connection.

This experience of serving and teaching others is much like Algebra II and trigonometry. It's hard work. It's not always going to make sense or be enjoyable, but the end result, after an extended period of time and patience, is worth it all.

Advanced mathematics causes you to think on a different level; it makes future problems seem easier to tackle, or at least helps us understand them better. It gives a feeling of accomplishment that you have endured and progress has been made.

As we took the conversation further, various students began to share their experiences with traveling. I realized their experiences were very limited, and probably should be. These were high school kids, with limited amounts of money and opportunities for such things.

With so many exchange programs, students have more chances to become involved in world travel at an earlier age. Educators must encourage kids to take hold of these opportunities.

Not only must educators encourage, parents must be willing to provide financial support. Most opportunities for travel are just too expensive for teenagers to handle by themselves. Without a family's support, it can be virtually impossible to fund a trip.

I give thanks for my family, friends, church, and even some complete strangers who have generously given of their money to support my journeys into other countries. Traveling to three countries (Jamaica when I was eighteen, Australia when I was twenty, and Trinidad when I was twenty-two) changed my life.

These experiences have helped shape the person I am today. And without the help of others, none of it would have been possible.

I don't really think my kids understood the hows or whys of my mini sermons on the importance of travel. I am sure they are still wondering why I would give up my vacation to do mission work and receive no pay for the hard hours of labor. This is a hard concept to understand and it is very difficult to explain.

But I think St. Augustine said it best when he stated, "The world is a book, and those who do not travel read only one page." One day I think traveling will be a reality for some of these kids, and maybe then they will better understand its importance.

The mediocre teacher tells. The good teacher explains. The superior teacher demonstrates. The great teacher inspires.

And Then Came Evaluations

18

"Take out a pencil or pen, and clear your desks please," I said as I walked up and down, in and around the students' seats.

"Miss Ledford, I hate pop quizzes. Why didn't you tell us? Do we need a sheet of paper? Are you gonna drop our lowest grade? Is this a test grade or a daily grade?"

All these questions, along with the slamming of books and various moans and groans, echoed around the room after my small request was made.

"No, you do not need a sheet of paper. I have provided everything you will need. And to answer all your moans and groans, this is not a pop quiz—not even close. I have prepared a teacher evaluation for you to complete, based upon my teaching abilities during this course, and other items of interest. This evaluation is very important, if not the most important thing you will complete this year for me.

"This written evaluation is your chance to grade me, so to speak, on my performance for this class. I want you to read the questions very thoroughly and spend ample time replying to each item. Please remember that you have plenty of time, so there is no need to rush through it.

"I want you to report on the good, the bad, and the ugly that you have experienced as a result of this class. I take these evaluations very seriously and I want you to do the same. I view this opportunity much like voting: you are given a chance to express your views and feelings toward what you have encountered, and now is the time to cast your ballot.

"I use your comments, remarks and suggestions to improve this course and myself. I am always striving to better this class, and without your help it will be virtually impossible. If you do not vote, so to speak, or cast your ballot of comments, then there is no room for complaint about or applause for my performance. You are denying your given right to express your opinion of this course. So, please ... spend some time in thought before responding on paper.

"And lastly, do not sign the evaluation. It is not important I know who you are, but only what the suggestions are. Oh, and I promise, I will not stay up till midnight trying to match the handwriting so I can really see who said what—all of that is totally irrelevant to me. Speak your mind, but be truly honest with each comment.

"Are there any questions?"

"Miss Ledford, do we get extra points if we write all good things and sign our name so you'll know who we are?" asked one of my more mischievous students who was hanging onto a 70 average by the skin of his teeth.

"No, William, you will not receive extra points for 'brown-nosing.' This is for my benefit only, not for yours. Now get to work so you can get all of the questions completed."

As the period came to a close, the papers began to come in. Some students seemed to have a look of satisfaction in their eyes as they laid their papers on my desk. Others seemed exhausted by the process of having to think back on what had taken place over the course of the year. And, well, a few just seemed glad that it was over.

By the end of the day, 138 evaluations had been received. I eagerly packed them away in my bag. My greatest homework task of the year is ahead of me tonight, I thought, as I straightened the room and put an end to my day.

☑   ☑   ☑

The results of these evaluations were interesting. Here is a sampling of what I read as I sifted through them, question by question.

Mind you, I have not changed any of the wording; these are exactly as they were written by the students.

Question 1: Do you think this class has been well worth your time, energy and effort? Why or why not?

- Yes, because I have learned in here. When you go out of a classroom and know much more than you did before you came in here, you can say it was well worth your time.

- Yes, I do think that this class was well worth my time. This class is not a crip course like everyone thinks it is. I found this class very educational.

- Yes. This class has helped me learn things about the "real" world.

- Yes. Because I like this class because it had some hands-on experience.

- Yes, this class has definitely been well worth my time and energy. This class has gotten me through some of the hardest times this year.

- Yes, because I have learned more than people think I have with Miss Ledford.

- Yes. It helps me get along with others. It's the kind of class to where everyone participates.

- Yes, at first I thought the class would be a bore, but after you get used to it you try harder and you make me use my brain and all of my energy.

- Yes, because I think I will use the material later when my baby arrives.

- Yes, because we had fun, but we also learned while having fun.

- Yes, I thought at the first of the year that this would be an "easy A" class but I have realized that I was wrong. I have thoroughly enjoyed working for my grades and I learned a lot.

- Yea, I guess because it's a good class and a good teacher and she likes to get right down to the nitty gritty.

Question 2: How did you like the class which was taught by Miss Ledford? Were the topics interesting and enjoyable to you?

- The topics were very interesting. You taught stuff I never knew was taught in Home Ec.

- I liked this class a lot. The topics were very interesting. You had a story to tell for almost every topic and I like that.

- I loved the class (Home Ec. I) I thought that this would be nothing but a "crip" course! It wasn't though. I learned some real statistics on children having children that I could not believe.

- I liked it. I liked learning about making a budget, and learning how to dress for a job interview, because these are things that will directly affect me.

- I liked it a lot. The topics were very interesting and enjoyable. I liked cooking and sex education.

- I liked it! I thought all of the topics were interesting and enjoyable. I just hate reading.

- I really enjoyed this class. You showed interest in all students and did not have favorites. The topics were great.

- I enjoyed it a lot. I liked most of the topics covered. Not all of them, but nobody likes everything.

- It is the only class you can really relax in.

- I thought this class was my favorite all year. The topics were some that I had never learned about before. Usually by 7th period I would have been asleep, but I was eager to participate in the class discussions.

Question 3: What are some areas that need improvement in this course?

- It would be better if we had more time in this class, but other than that, there isn't too much to improve on.

- The class room is to dull. Paint it. Please!

- More activities and group work. I learn more from group work.

- We need to have the equipment fixed that needs it.

- Don't read as much. If so, read orally.

- Not much. Just be a little more loose with the class ... then you can catch the rhythm.

- Less work—you give us too much to do all the time.

- More time with each person, but I know that's hard to do.

- You need to shorten some of your lectures. Give shorter tests ... not essay all the time. Do not make us keep a notebook.

- I think you may need to be a little bit more organized because usually we waited on you before we started class, but other than that your a great teacher considering this is your first year here!

Question 4: List the 3 things YOU liked best about this course.

- I enjoyed the cooking time, Christmas projects, and especially hearing Miss Ledford's stories.

- Cooking, learning how to do laundry, Miss Ledford's tests (they were hard, they made you study)

- Money management, the relaxed atmosphere, and the group discussions.

- Games, videos, and the fun teacher.

- The unit on human sexuality, color analysis, and designing my dream home.

- Class projects, cute little computerized tests, and open class discussions.

- Not a lot of homework, not a "you do this" kind of class, and a teacher who cared.

- The way you reviewed us for tests, the positive environment in which the class was taught, and the freedom you gave to us.

Question 5: Please rate Miss Ledford based upon her attitude, enthusiasm, and teaching abilities.

- Miss Ledford is a great teacher. She knows what she's talking about and to me she seems to love teaching.

- On a scale from 1 to 10, I would give you a 9 ½ because you are really enthusiastic, have a good attitude, and you are a great teacher. The ½ mark I wouldn't give you because you talk too much.

- Miss Ledford is one of the best teachers in the school. She is friendly, energetic, and fun to be around. She seems like she loves to teach by the way she acts in class. She makes the class fun. She is also young and students can relate to her well.

- I'd give you a perfect 10 in all of the above. You always have a positive attitude and are always happy about something. You take your teaching seriously! I like that.

- Miss Ledford is a very wild teacher. She likes to talk and has some good stories.

- Miss Ledford is a good teacher. When I had a problem she'd be there to make me understand it better. Also she helped me get rid of a big problem in my life. I like that most about her. She's a friend.

- 10, but sometimes you're just too perky. You're starting to rub off on me.

- A+. I truly believe that in all my years (11) of being a student, I have never found a happier or nicer teacher. Home Ec is a great way to end the day thanks to you.

- Miss Ledford has a good attitude toward her job as our teacher. She was persuading us to do better. I may have acted terrible in her class, but I think she was fair to us.

- She has a good attitude, even towards disruptive students. She doesn't hold a grudge. She has a lot of enthusiasm towards teaching. Her teaching abilities are good. She can back what she says.

Question 6: I feel this instructor is an effective teacher. Yes or No.

- Yes. Her effectiveness on the pupils is very strong. A lot of students think she is a great teacher and can confide in her about personal problems.

- Yes. She puts a lot into her class, she always tries to get the point across and make everyone feel important.

- Yes. Because I have learned a lot of things about the business and real world in this class.

- You are a down to earth teacher; you act like one of us.

- Yes. If she hadn't been so hard on me to keep pushing I probably wouldn't have passed this year because all I wanted to do was play and she helped me.

- Yes. The way she shows that she cares about your future.

- Yes. You focus on things that are important. I think a lot of people listen to you more than other teachers because you focus on everyday problems.

- Yes. You have made a great impression on my life! This course has prepared me for what lies ahead. And all along I thought this course was for girls. Ha.

- Yes. Because I've learned a lot from her. She knows the right way to make you learn.

Question 7: I would enjoy taking another course from this instructor. Yes or no.

- Yes. I would like to take another course from Miss Ledford but 1 don't know if I will be able to because of my schedule next year.

- Yes. This was the best subject. My mom said she could even tell that I've learned a lot.

- Yes. Because I like how you teach and your not boring at all and you're crazy (in a good way).

- Yes. As a matter of fact I have signed to take her for 2 classes next year. She has a positive attitude towards all her students.

- Yes. The way you push your students is great! During class and clubs you want the best and you have made me strive to be my best at everything. You also go against my negative self-esteem.

- Yes. If I do take another course, I will try to get in a class that I don't have so many friends with. If I have a friend in the class, it is hard for me to pay attention.

Question 8: Please list any additional comments or suggestions you have for the Home Economics program.

- I have also enjoyed FHA this year. We were very active and I feel we deserve the award for the best club. Miss Ledford helped me see the good things in me.

- I'd like to thank you for everything you did for me and I hope you will keep FHA going strong. Thanks a lot.

- I think whenever Tiffany died you were a big help to me especially, but also to everyone else. You made time for us.

- It's a great class. I will suggest it to other students.

- Other than the hard tests, it has been the highlight of my junior year.

- You could have fund raisers to help raise money so you could buy more materials to teach class with.

- I'm sorry, but I don't like the essay tests.

- It's a good class and well worth a person's time. Very interesting class and there is a lot to learn. I took this class as an easy course and was definitely surprised. I'm glad I took the class because I got an award out of it, plus my dad was proud of me.

- I really love your class—it's one of my favorites. But we should have time for activities and more food labs.

- Do more fun things. Lighten up on the test questions, don't make them so hard.

- That we get to go on field trips to other schools.

This feedback from the students is what keeps me doing what I'm doing, but it is only part of the evaluation process. The administrative evaluation is the part that scares most first-year teachers to death.

Tennessee requires three formal classroom evaluations by administrators. Sweating through these class periods builds stamina and character. Nonetheless, these are grueling times for the inexperienced teacher who doesn't know exactly what to do or expect.

Each evaluator is a bit different in his or her method of rating. What the evaluator thinks is good teaching is all that really matters.

Knowing what lay ahead for me, I decided to take the bull by its horns and wrestle it to the ground. And I did just that. I went to the administrative office and signed up for my first evaluation. I wanted to get this over with as quickly as possible.

As my first evaluation was about to begin, I said a little prayer and started the class promptly. I began with the roll call and proceeded to my introductory remarks.

As Mr. Thomas peered out at me through the half-on, half-off glasses perched on his nose, my nerves began to tighten. My throat felt as if I had swallowed a jar of cotton balls and I began to feel restricted in my speech.

What is he writing down? I thought to myself as I tried to remain focused on the day's lesson plan. Have I already blown it this early in the process? Or is he commenting on how well organized I seem to be?

Whatever he was doing, it was becoming a bit distracting. I no longer was concerned about the lesson, I was enthralled with how I was doing or what grade I was making, so to speak.

I was acting like the kids; just me give me my grade, that's all I'm concerned about. Surely I had not fallen a victim or regressed to acting like a sixteen-year-old who was cold and indifferent to the learning process and only concerned about the grade ... or had I?

The end of the class finally arrived. I was never so happy to have successfully finished a class as I was this one. However, Mr. Thomas continued to write. He did not look up. He acted as if the class was still in progress.

Did I quit too early? Did I dismiss the class to an empty hall just to have this whole thing over with? If I shouted at the top of my lungs, "It's over!," would that capture the attention of my evaluator?

It seemed as if days had passed when Mr. Thomas arose from his chair in the back part of the room and said, "I'll talk to you about this tomorrow during second period."

With that muffled comment, he was out the door.

Talk to me about what? How well I did for a first-year teacher? How horrible the lesson was? How well I used time management and controlled the students' behavior? About what? Not even a reassuring comment that everything was going to be all right?

Now another sleepless night was in store as I pondered the meeting we would have the next day. At this point, I just wanted this whole process to magically disappear so I would not have to go through with the follow-up session.

Tomorrow did come, but not a moment too soon. As I walked the short distance to Mr. Thomas' office I tried to gain some confidence.

The short walk seemed like a long journey.

"It can't be that bad," I said, reassuring myself with each step as I neared the door, "but it probably isn't going to be good either."

Oh well, my time had come.

"Good morning, Mr. Thomas. How are things going?"

"Fine, just fine. Why don't you take a seat and I'll be right back with your chart."

Going to get my chart? Now I felt as if I was a nine-year-old in the doctor's office waiting to hear if I was going to get a shot or medicine. The anxiety of waiting to see the outcome was more than my nerves could handle. But I continued to pray for medicine. Please go easy on me since this is my first experience; don't give me an injection that will cause too much pain, I thought.

Mr. Thomas retrieved the chart and entered the room with quite a determined look on his face.

"First of all, concerning your Unit Plan ... you will need to rework it. Your objectives and strategies seem to be running together. This plan is much too detailed and very lengthy. Be concise and shorten the plan. Take out some of these things that are not absolutely necessary. Spend some time with it and turn it back in to me within a couple of days."

In my mind I was fighting the urge to say, "This is a unit I made an 'A' on in college, and even the professor wanted a copy for his files as a future example to show other students; now I'm actually out in a school with a real teaching job and in an evaluation process that requires all of these guidelines and it does not meet their standards."

I could not believe my ears. What I had learned in college was a huge contradiction to what I was now being asked to put into effect as a first-year teacher.

"Moving right along," he continued, "I have made various comments regarding your lesson plan, class presentation and classroom management. Look these over and then sign on the space provided. Your signature does not mean you necessarily agree with your rating or comments, but that you have reviewed this with me.

"Also, there is a space here for any comments you may have (long pause). Oh, I just wanted to commend you on your enthusiasm and zeal portrayed to your students. You have a great rapport with them. That's one of the best things you have going right now.

"Keep up the good work. Get the unit plan turned in and we'll schedule your next evaluation."

"Thanks, thanks for your time. I'll get that to you right away," I responded as I gave a firm handshake and left.

As I walked back to my room, this incident reminded me of when my mother used to give me the whipping of my life, and then give me a big, fat, juicy hug with words of encouragement that everything was going to be all right.

"It hurts me worse than it does you," she would say. "It's just a necessary part of being a parent."

I was never really sure what to make of her rule of conduct. Now I know it was all just part of trying to smooth things over till the next time.

And the next evaluation finally arrived, and the next. Through this long process of being graded, I was learning a lot about myself and the system.

I did need to improve various aspects of my teaching, and I began to see great results after I did so. In fact, I think my teaching abilities increased a notch or two due to the feedback I was receiving.

On the other hand, the process of evaluation is lacking in some areas. The system (forms, requirements, outline structure, etc.) is set up on the same criteria across the board. Regardless of the curriculum being taught, teachers are evaluated in much the same way, which can be quite biased.

For example, the TIM model of lesson planning does not fit so well with the type of lessons I may teach on any given day in the varied curriculum of vocational home economics.

So what does a teacher do? He or she uses a lesson that can be adapted to the TIM model on days when evaluators are present. Thus the evaluator sees what he wants to see.

The reason we do things like this is to make a good score on the evaluation, which will be on permanent record in our file. And, believe me, playing games like this is time consuming and stressful for a teacher.

☑   ☑   ☑

The final part of this process is what I call "self-evaluation." I feel this analysis is the most difficult because it requires honesty, time, and the ability to see yourself clearly for who you really are. It's difficult to stop and say to yourself, "You goofed ... you blew it!," but there is a tremendous amount of satisfaction when you can honestly say, "Boy, that really worked. Those kids really learned, and I was a part of that learning process."

This is a healthy ritual that takes endurance and stick-to-it-ness. Examining yourself is like baring your soul to an audience of strangers, if you do it right. It's taking a non-biased view of what you are doing, or accomplishing, be it good or bad. And then working like crazy to improve the bad and make the good even better.

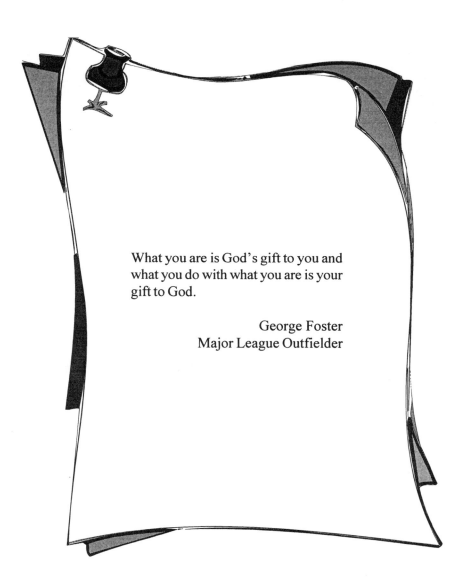

What you are is God's gift to you and
what you do with what you are is your
gift to God.

George Foster
Major League Outfielder

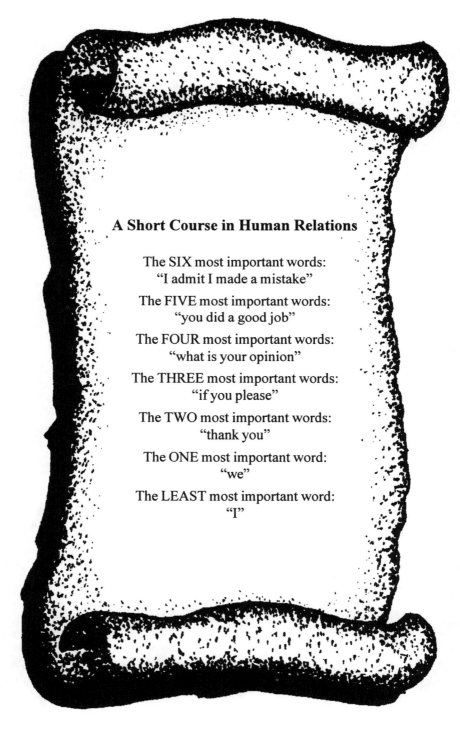

A Short Course in Human Relations

The SIX most important words:
"I admit I made a mistake"

The FIVE most important words:
"you did a good job"

The FOUR most important words:
"what is your opinion"

The THREE most important words:
"if you please"

The TWO most important words:
"thank you"

The ONE most important word:
"we"

The LEAST most important word:
"I"

Learn the Principles of Your Principal

19

I knew I had hit country when I first saw the boots. I'm still not sure what type of leather they were, but I do know they were 100 percent pure, authentic cowboy boots.

With his boots resting on the corner of his desk, we swapped some brief remarks. The further we went into the initial interview, the more I learned about my potential new boss and his boots.

The boots were not new by any means. Don't get me wrong, they were polished, but you could see the indentations and scratches that told a story of hard work and labor. They were made with genuine leather and stitched with the tightest and strongest of threads. They had a look of quality and sturdiness, able to withstand the test of time. They were quite ordinary in color and style, but had a sense of flare to them.

As I was mentally noting these specific traits of the boots, I noticed a strong parallel between the boots and the man wearing them. He looked ordinary, but had a sharp and polished aura about him. Through our brief conversation, I knew he was a man of hard work and strict discipline, a man who allowed only the finest individuals to be the leaders of his school, a school where he had "roped" his way to the top.

I learned more from this time together. He began to ask me questions about discipline techniques, teaching styles and extracurricular interests. He was trying to pry me open and find out if I was the type of leader capable of handling a group of high school kids.

I tried to stay relaxed and present an at-ease disposition. But his pointed questions kept me on the edge of my chair.

"So, why do you want to teach at Whiteville High School?" he asked.

"I want to put my four-year degree and the desires of my heart into practice. Due to lack of career opportunities, I have been in a dead-end job for the past year. Since there is an opening here, I want to take hold of it. I am so eager to finally get to teach, and I will give no less than 110 percent at all times."

With that answer, the boots hit the floor and he edged to the corner of his seat. He grew more intense from that point in the conversation.

He began to share his philosophy and beliefs for success at Whiteville High School. I was absorbing this information like a sponge, for I somehow knew this would be my "home away from home" for the next school year. You can call it luck, coincidence, foresight or a premonition, but I walked away from the interview with a positive feeling I would get the job.

That interview was thorough. I think we covered everything from A to Z (as I will do in Chapter 21), and then some. But I left knowing exactly what he expected, and it was up to me to decide if I wanted to take a shot at it.

And, of course, I did. But I couldn't wait to see if the boots remained. It is amazing how much you can learn from a person's appearance. Sometimes you get positive insights, other times negative ones. I think the outer appearance gives you specific information about an individual right from the start.

At each meeting thereafter, the boots were the center of his attire. Maybe it was just because he liked boots, or maybe because he knew he could make the look work at this small, rural school.

One day it was brown boots, the next black, ostrich skin one day, snakeskin the next. Tanned leather, natural leather, dried leather— you name it, he had it, and I continued to be amused that my principal wore them every day.

🥾 🥾 🥾

During this first year, I had a great working relationship with my principal. He was very helpful, supportive and well-informed about my classes and programs. He dropped by my room quite often just to make sure everything was OK.

But the key to making this relationship so successful was knowing that my principal was the boss. This was a hard concept for me to learn, but once I became accustomed to this type of authority, I adjusted easily.

It is so important to know your position and rank in your school. I was a first-year teacher, low on the totem pole, a true nobody who was nontenured and, believe it or not, I accepted it rather quickly. It is much easier to function within the system once you realize how much say-so you really have in a school. For me, it was very little.

So many bright, vibrant college graduates think that they can quickly land a job, come in and rule the school. It just doesn't happen that way. If you want to remain friends with your colleagues, I suggest you take a back seat to the more experienced teachers and draw from their knowledge and expertise.

In my experience, the old saying, "It's easier to ask for forgiveness than permission," does not apply in teaching (or at least at Whiteville High School). My principal always stressed the importance of open lines of communication, including asking about or discussing issues before they arose, not after.

It was not that he would deny most requests; it was just that he wanted us to observe the proper chain of command. Lines of authority were clearly set and he wanted us to follow the proper order when communicating.

He was adamant that you get his stamp of approval before proceeding with any special course of action. He stood firm and expected teachers to abide by this request. On occasion, someone would fail to oblige Mr. Shipley in this manner, only to their detriment.

Looking back on the year, my advice is to follow, or at least come to a compromise regarding, the dictates of your principal. Even if you do not wholeheartedly agree with his decisions, administration lines are the lines that run the school.

My principal was definitely the big fish in the small pond that was our school. He enjoyed the power of being principal and liked the idea of being in charge of a small school in a quaint little community.

He was previously the school superintendent for nine years, so he was accustomed to being in a powerful leadership position. And regardless of where your boss (principal) is or where he has been in previous years, you must respect his position.

Loyalty, honesty and sincerity are the three key elements in making this teacher-to-principal relationship work. It is vital to uphold these strong character traits.

Each day when I arrived at school I was representing Jada Ledford, and I felt it was necessary to uphold these values when dealing with my principal, other faculty members and students. Personal integrity is important, even in the midst of a disagreement or battle with administrators, because you never know when your paths will cross again.

I say all of this to try and bridge the gap that exists between so many teachers and their principals. Sometimes this relationship can mean the difference between having a good year or a bad year. With all the problems a teacher has to deal with, the last thing he or she needs is to have internal opposition from the principal.

By working faithfully eight hours a day, you may eventually get to be a boss and work twelve hours a day.

Robert Frost

I don't know the key to success, but the key to failure is trying to please everybody.

Bill Cosby

Three good reasons for being a
teacher: June, July, & August

...And Summer Finally Came

20

As teachers, we've all had the kid whose name we mumble under our breath, who was either the class clown or was just plain obnoxious for the entire year. This is a kid who is always causing a disturbance and making our jobs even more stressful.

Each year we will always have at least one Mitchell Watts, Chris Moore, Sarah Jenkins or Tonya Brown. There must be an unwritten clause somewhere that these unique creatures will always be a part of your classroom.

There is an atmosphere of drudgery surrounding the class he or she happens to be in, and we live for the minute when that class is over. It's not that you dislike this type of kid; it is just a relief when your time together each day is completed.

I had a couple of these kids my first year, and they are the kids I will never forget. Day-in and day-out they tried to do everything possible to cause havoc for me and the rest of the class, especially during those last few days when classes would seem eternal—surviving was just about more than I could stand.

Was I ever glad when summer finally came.

For me, trying to end the school year was much like trying to take down the Christmas tree and put an end to the month-long festivities December brings. I look forward to getting the tree, ornaments, and other decorations packed away so I can get my house back in some kind of order, but I am also saddened when the hype and activities are over.

All the rushing around and busyness of the season is very stressful, but enjoyable. I always want to extend the holiday, enjoy one more cup of Russian tea while singing Christmas carols with friends, and read the Christmas story one last time as we gather with the family for a time of prayer. But time moves on, and within a few short days a new year has begun.

The same goes for teaching. I couldn't wait till summer finally came so I could get everything filed away and get my classroom back in order. But there was a sadness that came over me when I realized I would not see my kids tomorrow, or the next day, or the next. No more lectures, discussions, games, FHA activities or projects for about ten weeks.

I wanted to have one more class with my seniors, give them one last piece of advice, and cherish those final minutes together. But the year was over—I had to look ahead and prepare for the next. And as hectic as the year had been, I was doing what my heart longed to do. I was fulfilling my mission in life.

I guess I was shocked more than anything that I was having these mixed emotions. I had told myself and everyone else I came into contact with in the last six months that I was living for May 28th to arrive. I wanted and needed a change of pace. It was obvious I needed a break, both physically and emotionally.

What I thought was going to be a long, restful summer turned into a saga of coaching basketball camps and attending conferences for professional development. I left the day school was out to attend a leadership conference in Nashville, and came back home to face two days of laundry before it was time to start the first of four week-long basketball camps.

Don't get me wrong; I enjoyed the coaching and learned a great deal more about the sport I dearly loved. And it was a different work schedule: no lesson planning, labs to prepare or papers to grade. But the camps did not satisfy me, and I started to feel more withdrawn than I had ever felt.

My life was thrown into a whirlwind when I received word there would be an available home economics position in Hamilton County, where I lived.

It was an eerie feeling to think that I could pack up and move from the school that had taken over my life for the past 180 days.

I began to grieve over the possibility of leaving. Even though the new position was the one I had longed for since college, I had become a part of this community. How could I turn my back on these people now? Doubts raced through my mind as I thought of the girls on my basketball team.

I had to keep a clear head, since this was an opportunity that might not come around again for several years. With few exceptions, home economics positions become available only when someone dies or retires. I had to consider this fact in my decision.

What a hard choice it was. After many hours of thought and several boxes of tissues, I made one of the toughest decisions of my life.

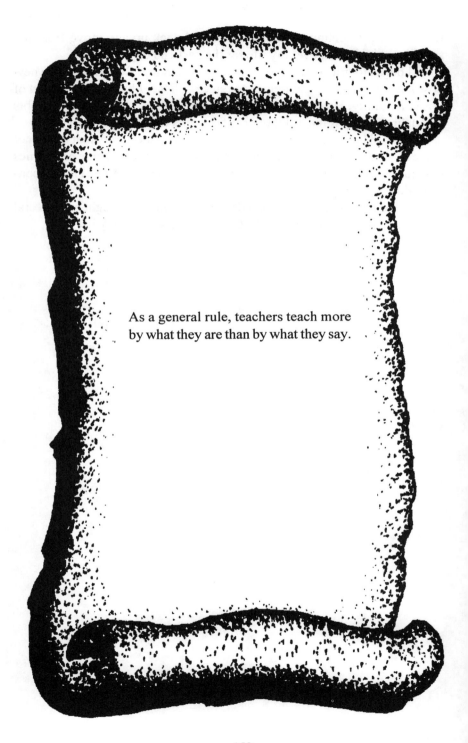

As a general rule, teachers teach more by what they are than by what they say.

The ABC's of My First Teaching Year | **21**

After a long year I found myself thinking back through events and memories of the 180 exciting days that had passed. It seemed like a form of regression to put my thoughts in an ABC format, but fitting, nonetheless.

A   **Attitude.** My mother has driven me nuts over the years, saying, "It's all in the attitude!" Every time I frown, feel sorry for myself or lose my motivation, Mom is always chanting her cliche. The scary part is that I found myself repeating those five uplifting words over and over again the whole year. It is a bit embarrassing to think your mother could actually be right about something. Thanks, Mom, for the many attitude adjustments you have given me over the years.

B   **Basketball, Basketball, Basketball.** This sport consumed me—my time, energy and enthusiasm were expended daily toward the game. Working with my girls was a true joy for me. The closeness we shared was a welded bond. As a coach, I learned many powerful insights that made me a better person.

C   **Coaching.** As the assistant girls' basketball coach, I received a $500 supplement for the year. Wow! I never realized coaching was so lucrative.

Conferences. In order to maintain a truly professional approach to teaching and stay well informed, I attended several conferences during the year. It was a marvelous time to broaden horizons and expand the world in which I lived. I suggest all new teachers take advantage of every opportunity to grow and learn new and exciting things.

Cafeteria. I have never eaten a better meal than what was prepared each day by our cafeteria staff. A homemade meal with at least two meat choices, three vegetables, a choice of bread, fruit, salad bar, a variety of desserts, and some of the best sweet tea I've ever had were items to choose from daily. No wonder most of us gained a few extra pounds over the course of the year. Lunch was one of the highlights in our school. Almost all of the faculty enjoyed this fine, country cooking every day, along with most of the students. Better yet, where else can you eat for $1.60?

D   **Daredevil.** You would have to be a daredevil to ever think of accepting a position in a high school. This past year reminded me of my childhood days when I played "truth or dare" with my friends. I always chose a dare, mainly for the adventure of it. And this year was one of the most challenging I had ever dared to partake in.

E   **Exciting, yet exhausting.** There was never a dull moment. For the most part I had a blast with the kids, and I have many happy memories I will cherish for years to come. But being so involved in the lives of your students can wear you out. I began to show signs of exhaustion early on, especially in the midst of basketball season.

F   **Fulfilling.** As hectic as things were, I pressed on to fulfill my lifelong goal of becoming a teacher. Being a teacher did something for me that no other job could do—it fulfilled my inner desires. What a great feeling to know that you are making a difference in the life of another human being.

FHA. I had an outstanding group of committed members in FHA. We grew close and developed some great, lasting friendships. We made a fine showing at our school, and I think we proved to be one of the best clubs going. Thanks to each of my members for such a successful year!

G   **Grades and Grade Cards.** There is nothing more time-consuming than averaging grades, especially since our grade cards were not computer generated. We had to follow the primitive method of going through stacks upon stacks of carbon copy grade cards to hand write each student's grade. This periodic event became a much-dreaded chore. Was I ever thankful that we were on the nine-week grading schedule!

H   **Homework (for me!).** As a first-year teacher, I carried home hours of homework to complete each night (lessons to plan, projects and papers to grade, labs to create, vocational reports to complete, and the list goes on and on). It was almost impossible to find time during the day to work on these things, and I soon found out that a teacher's day never really ends.

I   **Inconsistencies.** As I have said earlier in this book, my college preparation somewhat misled me as to what to expect when I went into teaching. What I had been taught and what was actually happening were two different things. But this continued to occur even within the school. One person would tell you one thing, another something else. For the most part, there are no hard and fast rules, no absolutes in teaching. I am a person who thrives on consistency. I like to at least know, in some sense, that things are operating on an even keel. However, I learned the only thing I could count on to be consistent was inconsistency.

J   **Juggling Act.** After this experience, I felt qualified to join "The Greatest Show on Earth" (you guessed it ... the circus). Learning to juggle my teaching responsibilities, coaching commitments, FHA club, church life, family life, dating and personal time was almost impossible. Trying to give the appropriate amount of time to each area became too advanced for even the best of jugglers. Making trade-offs and sacrificing what I wanted to do for what I had to do did not come easily to me.

K   **Kevin.** Even though he was just my boyfriend during this first year, he was my strongest supporter. I cannot possibly tell you of all the hours he spent in typing up tests, handouts, worksheets and letters so they would have a professional look. He was always there to cheer the girls on at the ball games and then drive me home, so I could get that extra thirty minutes of rest. And, most importantly, he was there to help me stay in one piece when my emotions would try to take over and get the best of me. Kevin, thanks for all you have done. It was so much fun sharing this with you.

L **Laughing.** It has been said that "laughing doeth the soul good." I would take this one step further and say "laughing is essential for the soul." Being able to laugh is a skill too few of us possess. From what I have seen, most teachers need to lighten up a bit and laugh more often. It's amazing how good it can make you feel. The process of laughing is like therapy—it is a positive way to deal with tension and anxiety build-up. So relax, learn to laugh at yourself, and enjoy laughter with those around you.

M **Meetings.** With the job of being a teacher comes a certain number of meetings. Faculty, vocational, FHA, professional and personal meetings with the principal are some of the powwows I was expected to attend. For the most part, these were very useful and informative. I guess meetings are a vital part of any job, regardless of how time-consuming they may be.

N **Noise.** High school kids are just plain noisy. Somewhere back in their preschool years they must have lost their inside voices. Kids like to carry on conversations with one another across the cafeteria, hall, room, or from opposite ends of the gymnasium. It is almost like they are yelling as they tell their stories. I'm not really sure where this practice originated, but it was a new concept for me as a first-year teacher. What ever happened to whispering?

O **Organization.** This tops my priority list. If a teacher is not organized, he might as well forget it. Kids expect you to be orderly and have a sense of direction about your teaching. Each day I worked so hard to keep everything organized but I found that, even as hard as I tried, there were days where I failed miserably. Keeping things filed so they will be accessible is a key to being organized.

P **Parents.** I learned early in my career that most parents want to be involved in their child's academic endeavors. Keeping open communication lines with the parents is the key to staying in control. Sending letters home, making brief phone calls, scheduling a conference, or taking the time to share a few words at a school-sponsored event goes a long way toward keeping your kids' parents involved with your program.

Q   **Questions.** High school kids could ask questions till the end of time and love every minute of it. I encourage my kids to do so, as the process helps to satisfy some of their probing curiosity toward the world in which they live. In my classes I always welcomed questions and, if I did not feel capable of making a sound, educated answer, I would research, make a phone call to a professional, or do whatever it took to bring back the proper information to the child. I found it amusing throughout the year to hear kids say, "Miss Ledford really knows what she is talking about, and if you ask her something that she doesn't know, you can be assured she'll find it out."

R   **Respect.** I was pleasantly surprised that these high school kids developed a great deal of respect for me. I had been warned by other professionals in the field, "Kids do not respect anything or anybody." I found this to be untrue. Of course, you are always going to have a few children who fit this category, but for the most part kids can be taught respect.

S   **Stressful.** I once read some magazine research that said teaching is the third most stressful occupation. After surviving this first year, I tend to agree with that finding. I think the main stress factor is the expectations placed on teachers. We, as a society, expect the schools to be fix-all institutions. Any social or political problem that emerges is blamed on the school system. Teachers are held accountable for much of our nation's stability, and this is a mighty large weight for most of us to carry.

T   **Teenagers.** I believe the 13-19 age group is the most perplexing group of individuals on Earth. The stage in the life cycle called adolescence is like a wild roller coaster ride. More changes are experienced in this period of a person's life than at any other time, and junior and senior high school teachers get to experience these changes firsthand, day-in and day-out. Teenagers are in a different world. These FLK's (Funny Looking Kids) dress, think, talk and act differently than any other creatures alive. It gets really interesting when you think you might have to get out the fly swatter to swat through the hormones floating around the room. Sometimes it gets so thick you really need a knife to cut through it. Even with all the kooky things that teenagers are going through, they are still a fun bunch of kids to be around. But I don't think everyone is cut out for this sort of work.

U   Unique. I had a unique experience this year. I was given the opportunity to teach home economics and coach basketball in a school very nearly the same size as my alma mater, Polk County High School. This small community reminded me of my childhood, and I developed a bond with the people. Teaching at Whiteville High School helped me rediscover who I was and, more importantly, who I was becoming.

V   Vacation. I lived for days off. Even a one-day vacation such as Labor Day was greatly anticipated. These short breaks were mainly a time for sleeping and cleaning house, since I was able to do very little of either during my regular workweek. I lived for the weekends so I could go see my family or catch up on my workload. And I could not wait to see the day summer would arrive!

W   Worried. I was worried all the time—worried I would not get everything turned in at the right time, worried if I would make it to school on time, worried I would not have time to get the groceries for food labs, worried about evaluations, worried about ball games, and the list goes on. I guess that's why I was diagnosed with an ulcer around mid-April.

X   "X"traordinary. There is nothing quite like the thrill of having your own class and being a "for real" teacher. All the training was finished, all my dues paid, and it was showtime. This extraordinary experience changed my life forever.

Y   You. One of the things I neglected this year was myself. If there is anything I want you to remember from this book, it is to make time for yourself. If you fall apart, your teaching suffers. Make it a priority to get plenty of sleep, eat a nutritious diet and get regular exercise. And, lastly, make time to do some things you enjoy.

Z   Zoo. It's a zoo out there! Need I say more?

Education is a social process ... Education is growth ... Education is not preparation for life ... Education is life itself.

John Dewey
American Philosopher/Educator

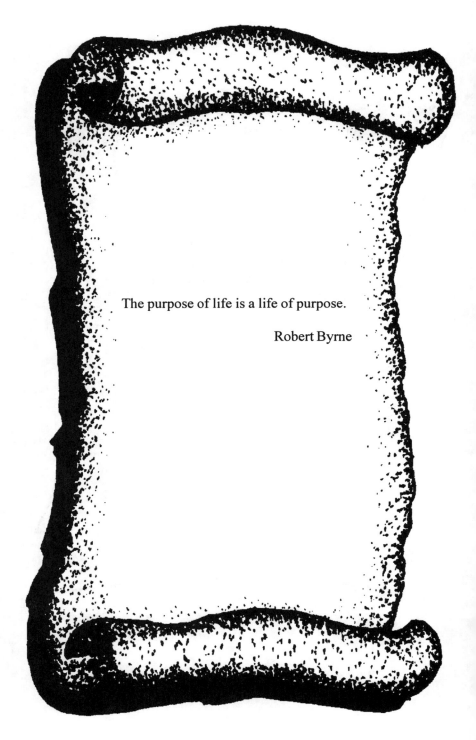

The purpose of life is a life of purpose.

Robert Byrne

Is Teaching Really for You?

22

"You don't have any idea what you're getting yourself into" was something I heard over and over again when I shared with others my desire to be a teacher. I was overwhelmed at the negative comments and discouraging remarks about the field I was driven to study.

Now that I'm finally here, I understand why these things were said. People should think seriously about teaching before they decide whether or not to pursue it. It is truly a mixed bag of good and bad. A person must do a lot of serious soul-searching before making a decision on whether or not to teach.

A teacher's job is much more complex than it appears on the surface. It is a powerful commitment to help in developing the lives of young people. If you do it right, you are on call twenty-four hours a day, seven days a week. It is so important to be available to these kids, not only for academics, but on a personal, one-on-one level.

I sit back and think about the evening Susan called with the news of Tiffany's death. Why did she call me? Because she knew she could, and because she knew I would have wanted her to. Kids need to know you care about them as individuals and that they have the freedom to call you if they need to.

I am a firm believer that teaching is not a science—it is an art. And because of this, I don't consider teaching a choice for everyone. I would almost go as far to say teachers are born, not developed or trained.

And speaking of training, the college education process for a teacher is a tedious one. I strongly urge all education majors to get out into the schools early, even before it is required in your courses. A person needs to visit area schools (public and private, city and county schools), sit in on some classes, talk to the teachers and meet with administrators, if possible. This will give you a more realistic view of what teaching is all about. I wish someone had advised me to do this, because I was unaware of how much high schools had changed in the short time since I had been a student.

Another thing I highly recommend is to be a substitute teacher for awhile. This will give you a first-hand view of teaching, how a school system operates, and how the kids respond to the educational process. You gain all of this knowledge while giving yourself time to reflect and decide if you want to do this full-time.

Substitute teaching is hard work, and you receive little pay for your efforts. But I think it is crucial to go through this grueling process so you will know what you are getting yourself into.

The junior and senior years are the most critical for an education major. You need to join educational associations, subscribe to education-centered literature, and go above and beyond what is asked of you as far as being an aide, tutoring, reading and research.

The more you expose yourself to the world of teaching, the better informed you will become. Keep abreast of political issues involving education at the local, state and national levels. Read a daily newspaper so you will stay up-to-date on activities and events concerning education.

But it takes more than this to be a great teacher. A person must possess some specific character traits to excel and be happy in this profession. The following are some questions you should ask yourself if you're serious about becoming an educator.

1. **Do you love young people?** If you don't like kids, then don't go any further. A teacher must enjoy the company of kids. On an average workday, you will be with approximately 140 to 160 kids, while sharing the company of only two to five adults. A teacher's job is totally invested in the kids. There must be a genuine bond of love for them or you will not last.

2. **Are you a patient person?** If you have a short fuse, volatile temper, or do not like to hear the words "wait a minute" or "what

did you say," teaching is not for you. Patience is a necessary quality for every teacher. It is the most important quality for a teacher to possess, particularly when dealing with special education or handicapped students.

3. **Can you take constructive or destructive criticism?** Everyone is not going to like you, regardless of what you do. Do not waste time trying to please everybody. It is not humanly possible.

   Believe me, criticism comes to every teacher at one time or another, be it during evaluations, parent-teacher conferences, meetings with the principal or confrontations with students. The key is how you decide to respond to it. Criticism can be a useful tool in making all of us better individuals, which makes for an improved school system.

4. **Are you a hard worker? Willing to stay at a task until it's completed?**

   I found out that teaching is not an easy job. It requires many hours of overtime with no additional pay. It takes a person with a stubborn work ethic to stay in education.

5. **Are you a team player?** You must be able to work closely with others in order to be a successful teacher. This may mean doing the dirty job no one else will do. It might also require allowing someone else to take the credit for a project or achievement, even if you should have been rewarded for it. And it could mean giving much more than you will ever receive. Being a team player is hard for some people, but a vital character trait for a teacher.

If you answered "No" to any of these questions, you might want to rethink your decision to be an educator. Even though this was just a sampling of things a soon-to-be teacher should think about, I feel they are some of the most important.

> "Life is like a box of chocolates—you never know
> what you're going to get."
>
> Forrest Gump

I relate this saying from the box office smash *Forrest Gump* to the life of a teacher. With each new year, new class and new day, you never know what lies ahead. Teaching is definitely an occupation that has an exciting life of its own. With never a dull moment to spare, it is oh-so-thrilling to break open that piece of chocolate to see what's inside.

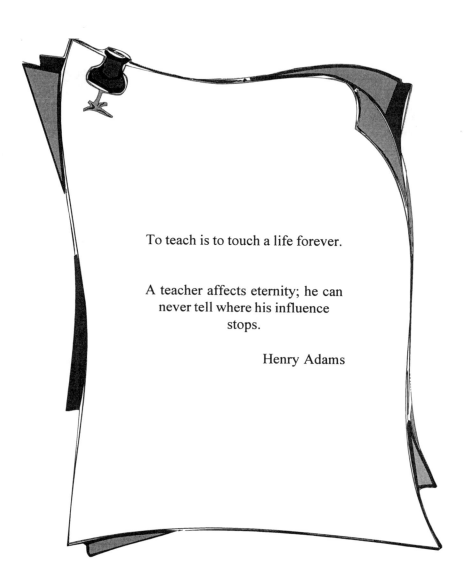

To teach is to touch a life forever.

A teacher affects eternity; he can
never tell where his influence
stops.

Henry Adams

Tough times don't last, tough people do.

Everyone who remembers his own educational experience remembers teachers, not methods and techniques. The teacher is the kingpin of the educational situation. He makes or breaks programs.

Sidney Hook
Education for Modern Man, 1946

It's So Hard to Say Good-bye

23

I did, in fact, accept the new teaching position. It seemed to be the only logical answer to my dilemma.

I wanted to teach in the county where I attended college and had chosen to make my home. I was frustrated with living in the Eastern Time Zone and working in the Central Time Zone—the juggling act was wearing me out as I arrived home late night after night.

Kevin and I were progressing toward marriage, and he had a stable job he had devoted more than four years to. It just seemed sensible to live in the county where we both were employed, attended church and paid our tax dollars. Also, this school change would cut my driving time to work in half.

Even with all these logical reasons to accept the job, I still had a difficult time with my decision. I endured many sleepless nights second-guessing myself. The hardest part was yet to come—breaking the news to my team.

Coach Barkley and I agreed to tell the girls in a group setting where we could all be together one last time. Since Sunday was the opening day of the girls basketball camp at our school, we decided this would be the most appropriate time to announce my plans to leave. The meeting would take place at 4:00 p.m. in the coach's office, with all girls being required to attend.

I arrived at school a little early to help ease my nerves. I had been sick to my stomach for the past two days and now I felt waves of extreme nausea washing over me. I was scared and very nervous. The closer it got to 4:00, the sicker I felt.

As the girls began coming into the gym, several came over and made jokes about me being late for camp.

"Where have you been, Coach Ledford? We missed you at the B-team game. We needed all the help we could get. Hey Coach, it's a good thing you weren't here to see me play ... it was awful. If you're not yelling at me, I can't seem to play as well."

These welcoming comments from this smiling, fun-loving group of girls made me feel good all over, but I had to excuse myself to the restroom so they would not see my tears.

Noticing the time, I tried to dry up and pull myself together. I was only five minutes away from telling my girls good-bye, and I wasn't sure if I could go through with it.

As I neared the office, I could feel the silence. All the girls were tightly nestled into the small space, with some even sitting on the floor. By the looks on their faces, I could tell they were not sure what this whole meeting was about.

Coach Barkley closed the door and nodded for me to take over. With his cue, I began.

"Well girls, we've called this meeting because I have some things I need to tell you. This is very hard for me; one of the most difficult things I've ever done in my life, and it hurts, but I am leaving Whiteville High School to take another job at a school in my county."

As tears streamed down my face it was almost impossible to continue. I looked up to see a bunch of teenage girls crying their eyes out. At this point I realized how much love there was between us.

Continuing, I said, "I want you to know this decision was not an easy one. It came about through many hours of crying and praying. I was put in a position where I had to make a quick decision, and I had to do what was in my best interest.

"There is a rare chance for me to gain employment in the county where I plan to continue my residence, so it's important for me to get tenure as quickly as possible. I just wish I could take all of you with me.

"I do want to say that you are absolutely the finest group of young ladies anyone could ever be associated with, and I was honored to be a part of this coaching staff. We have shared some great times together and I have many happy memories to cherish for a lifetime.

"I'll never forget you, I promise. You have impacted my life in a way you will never understand or possibly believe. I'm going to miss you dearly, and I'll especially miss getting to yell at you from the bench. But I'll be back; you're not going to get rid of me that easily. Kevin and I will be here to watch you play, and I'll probably be yelling from the stands. But I hope that's OK, because it will take some time for me to adjust."

We were all laughing and crying at the same time, and it suddenly became very quiet. I felt helpless because there was nothing else I could say or do to make the situation any better.

"Oh, and by the way, I plan to write a book about my time here at Whiteville High School, and you guys will be included. I'm very serious, girls. When I write the book, I will share about the team and some of the special circumstances we have been through together."

After that final comment, the girls began to shower me with big bear hugs and words of encouragement. They formed a line and I was able to spend a brief period of time with each player.

Tears continued to flow and tissue was passed around the room. The meeting resembled visitation at a funeral home, with lots of crying and softly-spoken words as each person came through the line.

I don't think I have ever been moved in that way before. I was experiencing one of the sweetest and most emotional times of my life, and I had given up a part of my world I was not sure I could live without. But the girls assured me we would stay close and be friends ... forever.

Endings are never easy. Whether it is ending a relationship with a boyfriend or girlfriend, going away to the military and saying good-bye to friends and family, or a high school graduation, it is always tough. It seems as though the hurt will never end and you wonder if the wounds will ever heal.

This speaks to me and says, "Jada, you'll make it—this part of your life will make you stronger and more capable of handling what will come next. Toughness is a character trait that can stand the test of time and allow a person to come out of the trial much better than they were before."

Leaving the school that nurtured me during my first year was devastating. The most difficult part was resigning the position of assistant girls basketball coach. I walked away from the meeting feeling I had let them down.

They had believed in me, respected me, and even looked up to me as a positive role model, and now I was turning my back on them. I lay in bed at night wondering if our paths would ever cross again.

I hoped I could move on, yet keep close ties to my girls and other students. And I did. But it is a most difficult thing to do.

It's kind of like when you have a one-sided breakup in a relationship and proclaim, "Let's be friends." You promise to call, visit and keep in touch, but it rarely happens. Friendship proves to be an uncomfortable thing, since there is no common bond. One person left the relationship against the wishes of the other. Confusion, hurt feelings, and a certain weirdness always accompany this type of situation.

I just hoped that this scenario would not prove true for me and "my girls."

The last thing I had left to do was to pack up my things. I worked in my department for a couple of hours pulling files, going through my desk and cleaning the room. As I muddled through my belongings, I came across several items that brought tears to my eyes.

One was a Hallmark card given to me by a student. It read:

> The ability to teach others is a special gift, and I want to thank you for sharing that gift with me ... You've made a big difference in my life.

She followed this with a handwritten note:

> Miss Ledford,
>
> I know you have only been teaching at WHS for one year, but I feel like I have known you much longer. You're a wonderful teacher and you have the ability to make learning fun and interesting.
>
> Some students go through high school never having the chance to be taught by someone with that ability.
>
> I guess what I am trying to say is, "You have really made a difference in my life and I will never forget you as long as I live."
>
> Love,
> Kristie Simmons, Class of 1993

Reflecting back on the year, I was awakened to all the wonderful experiences I had been a part of. Little notes and letters like this I had received on various occasions were proof I was doing the right job. Nothing speaks more clearly than words written by a student who has been touched.

I came across some funny things and found myself laughing out loud. And then I was frozen in time as I came across a picture of Tiffany that was taken during Christmas. I remember it so vividly.

We were decorating the room for the holidays and Tiffany found a string of miniature lights. She wrapped them in her hair and when she plugged them in it lit her up like a Christmas tree. She started singing, "O Christmas Tree" and "We wish you Merry Christmas" as she posed for a picture.

I yelled out to her, "Get those out of your hair, Tiffany. With as much hairspray as you wear, those lights might set you on fire. Hurry, take them out. We couldn't live without you!"

Memories like this cannot be bought. I had seen these events transpire, and now only my students and I could call them back in our minds to fondly remember again.

After everything was finally packed up, it was still hard to believe that I was leaving. I found myself pacing back and forth across my room, in and around the school, recognizing and committing to memory the sights, sounds and smells I encountered every day.

Never again would I enter those doors and walk down the carpeted halls of Whiteville High School as a first-year teacher. My time was over, I had served my initial year of service, and now I must place it down and walk away.

In the quiet of my heart and soul I whispered some personal sentiments as my final farewell. And, as I turned toward the door, the tardy bell sounded its alarm.

To this day, I think that was the school's way of telling me ... goodbye.

References

Bits & Pieces. (1986, June). *Arizona Association News.*

Children's Defense Fund, (1995). *A Vision for America's Future: An Agenda for the 1990's.* (p.xxxvi).

Children's Defense Fund, (1995). *The State of America's Children Yearbook 1995.*

Forrest Gump (1994). Paramount Pictures. Videocassette.

Making the Grade: A Report Card on American Youth, 1989.

Substance Abuse & Mental Health Services Administration, Office of Applied Studies. *1993 National Household Survey on Drug Abuse.*

Technology and the at-risk student. (1988, November/December). *Electronic Learning,* pp. 35-49.

Tennessee State Department of Education, Division of Vocational-Technical Education. (1990). *Home Economics Curriculum Framework for Tennessee.*

U.S. Department of Health & Human Services. (1990). *Vital Statistics of the U.S., Vol. II.* Mortality part A.

Wylie, P. (1942). *Generation of Vipers.*

TO PLACE AN ORDER

Telephone

USA/Canada:	**1-800-228-0810**
International:	**1-319-589-1000**

Hours: 7:00 am - 6:00 pm, Monday - Friday
(Central Time)

Fax

USA/Canada:	1-800-772-9165
International:	1-319-589-1046

Hours: 24 hours a day / 7 days a week

Mail

Kendall/Hunt Publishing Company
Kendall/Hunt Customer Service
4050 Westmark Drive, P.O. Box 1840
Dubuque, IA 52004-1840

We fulfill all orders within twenty-four hours of entry. If no shipping instructions are given, we determine the most appropriate method and ship accordingly. For individual orders, shipping and handling charges are $4.00 for the first book and $.50 for each additional book.

All individual orders must be prepaid. We accept Master Card, Visa, or American Express. Sorry, no C.O.D.'s.

Sales Tax: Orders being shipped to Alabama, Arizona, California, Colorado, Florida, Illinois, Indiana, Iowa, Kentucky, Louisiana, Maryland, Massachusetts, Michigan, New Jersey, New York, Pennsylvania, Tennessee, Texas and Wisconsin are subject to local sales tax unless a tax exemption certificate has been furnished to Kendall/Hunt.

Notes:

Notes:

Notes:

Notes:

Notes:

Notes:

Notes:

Notes: